CONTESTING 'RAC

In the decade since Kevin Hylton's seminal book *'Race' and Sport: Critical Race Theory* was published, racialised issues have remained at the forefront of sport and leisure studies. In this important new book, Hylton draws on original research in contemporary contexts, from sport coaching to cyberspace, to show once again that Critical Race Theory is an insightful and productive tool for interrogating problematic social phenomena.

Inspired by W. E. B. Du Bois' statement that 'the problem of the twentieth century is the problem of the colour line', this book sheds a critical light on the way sport perpetuates racism, while identifying opportunities to challenge its insidious presence. Exploring and explaining the ways in which notions of 'race' are expressed and contested at individual, institutional and societal levels, it addresses key topics such as whiteness, diversity, colourblindness, unconscious bias, identity, leadership, humour and discourse to investigate how language can be used as a device for resistance against racism in sport.

Contesting 'Race' and Sport: Shaming the Colour Line is vital reading for all sport studies students, academics and those with an interest in race, ethnicity and society.

Kevin Hylton is Head of the Research Centre for Diversity, Equity and Inclusion, UK and Professor of Equality and Diversity in Sport, Leisure and Education in the Carnegie Research Institute for Sport, Physical Activity and Leisure at Leeds Beckett University, UK. Kevin has published extensively in peer-reviewed journals and books, including *'Race' and Sport: Critical Race Theory* (2009); *Atlantic Crossings: International Dialogues on Critical Race Theory* (2011); and *Sport Development: Policy, Process and Practice* (2001, 2008, 2013). Kevin's research interests focus on diversity, equity and inclusion in sport, leisure and education. Kevin sits on the Editorial Board of the *International Review for the Sociology of Sport* and the *Journal of Global Sport Management* and is Co-editor of the book series *Routledge Critical Perspectives on Equality and Social Justice in Sport and Leisure*. Kevin is Patron of the Equality Challenge Unit, and Patron of Black British Academics.

CONTESTING 'RACE' AND SPORT

Shaming the Colour Line

Kevin Hylton

Routledge
Taylor & Francis Group

LONDON AND NEW YORK

First published 2018
by Routledge
2 Park Square, Milton Park, Abingdon, Oxon OX14 4RN

and by Routledge
711 Third Avenue, New York, NY 10017

Routledge is an imprint of the Taylor & Francis Group, an informa business

British Library Cataloguing in Publication Data
A catalogue record for this book is available from the British Library

Library of Congress Cataloging in Publication Data
Names: Hylton, Kevin, author.
Title: Contesting 'race' and sport : shaming the colour line / Kevin Hylton.
Description: Abingdon, Oxon ; New York, NY : Routledge, 2018. | Includes bibliographical references and index.
Identifiers: LCCN 2017042941 | ISBN 9781138885400 (hbk) |
ISBN 9781138885417 (pbk) | ISBN 9781315715476 (ebk)
Subjects: LCSH: Racism in sports. | Discrimination in sports. | Sports--Social aspects.
Classification: LCC GV706.32 .H949 2018 | DDC 306.4/83--dc23
LC record available at https://lccn.loc.gov/2017042941

ISBN: 978-1-138-88540-0 (hbk)
ISBN: 978-1-138-88541-7 (pbk)
ISBN: 978-1-315-71547-6 (ebk)

Typeset in Bembo
by Taylor & Francis Books

CONTENTS

TABLES

ACKNOWLEDGEMENTS

I would like to thank my partner, Pia, and my family for their support and love over the period of writing this book. Milli, Lukas and Lauren, as you embark on the next part of your journeys make each step count.

Thank you to Simon Whitmore and the team at Routledge Taylor and Francis for inviting me to write this book and for making another space for critical work in sport and leisure. In particular, my work on Critical Race Theory and that of others in the UK and beyond has benefitted from these opportunities to share with global audiences.

I would like to also thank academic colleagues and those involved in studies that contributed to the writing of this work. I am grateful for the contributions of key contacts and interviewees throughout which has been invaluable. The additional support of the National Offender Management Service for its contribution to Chapter 4 is much appreciated (now Her Majesty's Prisons and Probation Service).

Thanks as always to colleagues at Leeds Beckett University's Institute for Sport, Physical and Leisure, and my Research Centre for Diversity, Equity and Inclusion at Leeds Beckett. In particular, Emeritus Professor Jonathan Long, Dr Tom Fletcher and Dr Stefan Lawrence for your reflexivity in our academic pursuits that I considered further in Chapter 3.

I hope this work reflects and continues all of our conversations.

1

CRITICAL RACE THEORY IN SPORT

I am almost always aware of race, alert to its power as an idea, sensitive to its nuances in the world.

Arthur Ashe (1993: 138)

Du Bois (1994: 1) famously announced that *the problem of the twentieth century is the problem of the color line*. His words have not gone unheeded in sport and it is argued here that 'race' continues to be one of the most significant problems of the twenty-first century. There are relentless accounts of racism in sport that continue the relevance of these words within and without its domain. Yet Du Bois' idea of *the veil* hints at more than these overt manifestations of odious behaviours, it points to more subtle, systemic and structural racialised forms of oppression that require concentrated levels of critical consciousness to isolate, explain and disrupt.

Du Bois speaks of a double consciousness that he became aware of as a result of being Othered at a very early age. The outcome of early traumatic events led to him recognising that he was viewed differently by those racialised as White in the public domain. He argued that they drew on negative racialised behaviours, tropes and characteristics that delineated his identity from the majority White community just as Shuford (2001) more specifically describes 'race' as a construct for defining and locating people through imposed racialised categories, and for the allocation of resources. The veil signifies a position of racial consciousness for many that reveals the significance of 'race' in sport and society and the insidious nature of racism (Bell 1992)

For Du Bois, a 'veil' hung between him and the dominant whiteness that he experienced. It was emphasised by the privileges and supremacy of whiteness and those with the power to Other him. Living within the veil offered security and purview from which to observe and strategise how to navigate the racialised society outside. The veil also emphasised the racialised fractures found more generally across society where sport is but one contested domain (Winant 2004; Carrington 2013). Further, Du Bois' (1994) striving to become an African *and* an American is a pernicious fight against a forced hybridity that consequently leads to notions of 'them' and 'us', processes that include and exclude in the way that everyday business is regularly conducted (Werbner and Modood 1997; Giardina 2003; Ratna 2007).

Many scholars have argued for sport and 'race' to be taken seriously amid claims of it seamlessly mimicking dilemmas in other social settings. For example, sport's racialised dynamics affect, and are affected by, wider discourses, ideologies, structures, issues and controversies (van Sterkenburg, Knoppers et al. 2010; Burdsey, Thangaraj et al. 2013; Carrington 2013; Klugman and Osmond 2013; Testa and Amara 2016). The symbolism of sport for diasporic communities makes it more than whimsy (Burdsey, Thangaraj et al. 2013) and its analysis requiring a shift from the '*toy department of human affairs*' (Edwards 1979: 116) to a clear recognition that *sport matters* (Zirin 2007). Like Zirin (2007), Edwards (1979) supports the view of others today whom implicate sporting arenas in recreating and faithfully sustaining how racialised dynamics play out elsewhere (Lawrence 2014; Poulton and Durell 2014; Farrington, Hall et al. 2015). At the same time, sporting arenas are capable of challenging behaviours, attitudes and customs where thoughtful practice is harnessed (Long and Spracklen 2011; UN 2013).

Viewing the veil as a dialectic in sport, it can be argued that it not only reflects lived raced realities but can also signify the unstable and contradictory aspects of 'race' and sport (see Winant 2004). Hence, where there is racialised oppression and subordination there is the potential for anti-oppression work and empowerment. Where the veil is revealed institutionally the tensions of organisations and their actors must continue in a dynamic of resistance to these hegemonic forces. We have seen this in sport where moments of social or political resistance have revealed the subtle dynamics of the veil. Yet what these successes have regularly signalled in sport and society is the scale of the task of racial equality and 'race' which *continues to be the problem of the twenty-first century.*

Ashes to racism

When African American tennis legend Arthur Ashe described an interview with a journalist about how he was coping with AIDS he hinted at his own double consciousness, the veil and the prevalence of racism. Ashe wrote the following in a chapter entitled 'The Burden of Race' in his autobiography *Days of Grace*:

> I could see that she was groping for the right words to express her sympathy for me before she left … 'Mr Ashe, I guess this must be the heaviest burden you have ever had to bear, isn't it?' she asked finally. I thought for a moment, but only a moment. 'No, it isn't. It's a burden alright. But AIDS isn't the heaviest burden I have had to bear.' 'Is there something worse? Your heart attack?' […] 'Race has always been my biggest burden. Having to live as a

minority in America. Even now it continues to feel like an extra weight tied around me.'

(Ashe 1993: 133)

Ashe reached his conclusion about 'race' and AIDS because he contracted AIDS after a blood transfusion whereas he stated that his experience of racism … *is entirely made by people, and therefore it hurts and inconveniences infinitely more* (Ashe 1993: 134). Ashe was conscious of the effects of 'race' and racism growing up in the state of Virginia and despite his undeniable successes his psyche was marked as a result, and captured in the quote at the beginning of this chapter. However, Ashe's revelations are not unique in the biographies of sportspeople where 'race' and racism permeate this arena as much as the next.

In my inaugural professorial lecture I felt compelled to explain, even to a learned audience, that 'race' and racism are problematic in sport and society. A set move for most critical sociologists, but an important one to establish a starting point for the discussion that ensued. The term 'race' is significant for me not just as a socially constructed concept but as a significant ontological truth, which is why I use it in scare quotes. What that does is to signpost that it should not be read nor used uncritically. I refer to Omi and Winant's (2002) work on racial formations to describe how we must understand that 'race' is a paradox, that it has been decried as a fallacy by the United Nations, high ranking and influential organisations, politicians, and academics (UNESCO 1978; Carrington 2013; UN 2013; Hylton and Long 2016; IOC 2017).

However, challenging 'race' at one end as a non-existent fallacious concept or as a social construction at the other oversimplifies the fact that for many like Ashe the lived reality trumps these sociological concerns. I acknowledge the dilemma of 'destabilising the notion of race theoretically' while recognising 'the lived presence of 'race' (Fine, Weis et al. 2003: 176). In a racialised society, to reduce 'race' to an objective condition or to an ideological construct denies our everyday experiences which has become the basis for most of my work. So, for those who feel that talking about 'race' only perpetuates racism, consider Malcolm X's view that *Racism is like a Cadillac, they bring out a new model every year!*

Racism

The notion of racism is often misunderstood or viewed narrowly in sport resulting in inadequate responses to incidents, or with systematic and more subtle infractions being missed completely. Elsewhere I consider the everyday understandings of what racism is because it means different things to different people (Hylton 2009: 10). There are different descriptions of what racism is and how it operates. For Sue (2003) racism is a mix of attitudes, actions, structures or policies that lead to the subordination of people due to colour or culture. Westwood (1990) signals that mistakenly held beliefs of natural racial superiority reinforce assumptions of racial dominance and underpin rationales for maintaining hegemonic racial hierarchies.

While Trepagnier (2010) goes as far as to conclude that some social groups think about racism in different ways. White people are more likely to think of racism in binary opposites of 'racist or not racist' which in both cases ignores the unintended systematic nature of racism which, not surprisingly, Black people are more likely to be persuaded by, however. Racism can be viewed existentially as a 'felt' individual or group experience; it is a noun that names stigmatising processes; it is ignorance of other cultures; it is a concept with little analytical credibility; it is a concept that differs over time and space; it is a phenomenon that intersects with other axes of power; it is systemic; it is not aberrant; it is structural. Holland (2012: 3) agrees that Critical Race Theory sees *racism as ordinary*; she goes on to to state that *racism is almost always articulated as an everyday occurrence, as pedestrian rather than spectacular.* What racism is, and how we can best understand and challenge it, is a worthy undertaking for key stakeholders in sport.

Definitions of racism tend to have certain characteristics in common. They stress the prevalence of racialised ideologies of superiority, prejudice and power while reinforcing the notions of exclusion, subordination, and subjugation of racialised and minoritised others. Solorzano, Miguel et al. (2000) identify three important points in definitions of racism: (1) one group believes itself to be superior, (2) the group that believes itself to be superior has the potential to carry out the racist behaviour, and (3) racism affects multiple racial groups. Racism is a worldwide phenomenon and is not isolated to the West or historical imperialist colonisers, it is not one but a multiplicity of manifestations and experiences, it presents itself in different forms, in different contexts, with varied histories and politics that shift over time and place (UN 2005). This dynamic can be viewed in Anthias and Yuval-Davis' definition of racism in its plurality when they state that,

> Racism(s) need to be understood as racialised ... Modes of exclusion, inferiorization, subordination and exploitation that present specific and different characters in different social and historical contexts
>
> *(Anthias and Yuval-Davis 1993: 2)*

I am not repentant for doing work in this area; I do not hold on to the hope that I will stop talking about 'race' and racialised dynamics in sport and society too soon. But we must remember that *Peace won't be still of its own free will*, and if those words were poetic enough for Gil Scott Heron then they are good enough for me!

'Race' and sport: whose story?

Dominant epistemologies in sport and leisure theory, policy and practice are very powerful and yet it is important to ask *Whose story is it?* Whose knowledge is included and who/what is excluded from research? For example, one story of 'race' and sport can be a very liberating one. One that would state that 'sport is a meritocratic, colourblind, equal opportunities site of social relations where diversity can meet and people, possibly for the first time, can begin to accept each other for who they are. Playing together, integrating, cohering … in fact sport becomes this "cultural glue" that binds us within and across groups. Prejudices dissipate, community is strengthened and society functions more smoothly.' This is the dominant story of sport and its benefits which most of us may have succumbed to at some stage.

Another story could be that through sport our social divisions are reinforced as hierarchies are maintained, remain monocultural and assumptions about the 'other' are left unchallenged. Post-'race' arguments of meritocracy obscure the racial processes that emerge and aggregate, as microinsults, microassaults and microinvalidations become a matter only of ad hoc concern for key stakeholders. These are issues that continue to exercise the mind of critical race scholars and push them to find better and more insightful responses to these concerns.

Du Bois (1994: 1) would describe me as *bone of the bone and flesh of the flesh of them that lives within the veil*; I do not say this in a way of articulating an aggrandised way of being, but rather one that reflects how I navigate places and spaces. Being a Black British-Caribbean, straight, able-bodied, adopted northerner, from the East End of London, and male, I am in a constant state of reflexivity and consciousness. Either implicitly or explicitly I rarely have an interaction that is not subtly racialised in some way … whether the scenario is impacted by the past, present or what I am likely to do in the future. Tate (2016: 73) describes this state of 'affect' as *racism's familiar invisibility*. Further, in my teaching over the years in sociology, sport, leisure, community and education, I have always had to consider how questions raised about 'race' have had to be carefully constructed for my predominantly White students so as not to draw questions about my motives for discussing issues relating to 'race' and social inequalities. This denial of standing for the Black voice on 'race' and racism is reflected in the diversity of knowledge formers and leaders in sport and the academy (Bell 1992; Carrington 2012).

Denied standing also operates when the notion of a 'Race Card' is deployed to describe stealing an unfair advantage over others because of 'race'. What many do not consider is that the idea of the 'Race Card' invalidates real experiences of racism by trivialising and objectifying them. 'Playing' the 'Race Card' suggests that structural obstacles and everyday microaggressions are excuses. Reducing racism to inconsequential and strategic game playing renders 'race' irrelevant. There is a strong possibility that some seeing my inaugural lecture online or reading this book will argue that I am evidence that there are no obstacles in sport, leisure and education, and that some people use the 'Race Card' as an excuse for *not* progressing or working hard enough. To those people I say this, I remember Kim Crenshaw, a central figure in CRT, saying that sometimes she leaves work to find that she is exhausted not just from her work but also the performance of what scholars describe as whiteness. One cannot play at being a racialised individual and neither is racism a game that anyone would wish to play. This performance can be wearisome. Yet in sport we can see that the conspicuous nature of whiteness or even perceptions of who can succeed in a particular environment, whether practical or academic, can cause a haemorrhaging of highly productive colleagues (Press Association 2017).

I have been a [full] professor for a number of years now and yet I am one of only a few Black professors in the UK (Alexander and Arday 2015). That says much about the education system in the UK, and in sport and leisure studies that figure drops down to just one. This might explain why the perception of the 'knowers' in sport and leisure do not necessarily look like me and that what is 'known' in dominant epistemologies does not necessarily reflect my experiences.

Such issues are symptomatic of my work. Not only this, my research has incorporated an ongoing pursuit of revealing the dangers of racialised dynamics; improving our theoretical and methodological approaches to these and related issues; while offering a challenge to academics and practitioners to locate themselves within these processes of power so that they become part of the solution to complex racial issues. On this note, in 1934 W. E. B. Du Bois (1998) wrote in *Black Reconstruction in America (1860–1880)* that stories are influenced by two views: one that believes racialised others are ordinary beings who under fair circumstances can develop like anyone else, and a second that holds on to notions of inferior others, that therefore require different sorts of answers. If you are reading this book and the second view is held then you will need more than the ideas I discuss in this book … Like Du Bois I am not trying to convince those people … I assume the truth of the first (Du Bois 1998: 1).

Critical Race Theory

The praxis of CRT reminds me of two observations. One came from Martin Luther King Jnr, who said *In the end we will not remember the words of our enemies but the silence of our friends*, and the second is a comment from (Hutnyk 1997) who argued that, *It is well and good to theorise the diaspora, the post-colony and the hybrid but where this is never interrupted by the necessity of political work it remains a vote for the status quo*. Critical Race Theory signals the incompleteness of sport and leisure theorising and practice where broad discussions on 'race' have inconsistently factored-in these social issues (Hylton 2005; Hylton 2010; Hylton and Morpeth 2012; Hylton and Lawrence 2016). Yet CRT can be used as a cross-disciplinary compass to guide a critical approach to sport and leisure analyses. An approach to sport and leisure that has had me transfixed by what Gaertner and Dovidio (2005) would describe as the tension between public commitments to equality, systemic discrimination and bigotry, and the ongoing struggle against racialised inequalities and disparities.

Using the metaphor of a camera, Zamudio, Russell et al. (2011) and Solorzano (2013) emphasise the essential elements of a critical social theory. Solorzano (2013) argues that theory is like a polarising filter in a camera that focuses the eye to eliminate the glare from a window so that we can see what the eye cannot. Zamudio, Russell et al. (2011) use the notion of theory as a model to frame and interpret society like a good photographer's image that omits extraneous detail. Using CRT to see a problem clearly, and therefore to see through that problem, is the role of any critical theoretical tool. Where Zamudio, Russell et al. (2011) agree with Solorzano (2013) that *a theory is a lens through which we observe and interpret social life* Solorzano (2013) goes further to stress that a pure concentration on observing and interpreting is not likely to bring substantive change. He proceeds to the conclusion that,

> CRT is an explanatory framework that accounts for the role of race and racism [and] works toward challenging racism as part of a larger goal of identifying and challenging all forms of subordination.
>
> *(Solorzano 2013)*

Critical Race Theory in sport enables a concentrated focus on racialised problematics. CRT is a useful tool to reveal a clearer understanding of the dialectic of 'race', sport and society to facilitate a critique of complex personal, cultural, institutional and structural arrangements. Where racialised processes, formations, meanings and consequences are of concern CRT can function as an organising critical framework from which to focus our approach to them. Where we have the ability to see the racism, racial inequalities and disparities that litter our everyday interactions in a more sophisticated and nuanced way, we are more likely to reveal solutions and challenges to them.

There are core tenets or assumptions that are frequently cited that help to define CRT. Though some activist scholars will focus on some more than others, there are common tenets cited in each case:

1. The centrality and permanence of 'race' and racism and their intersections with other forms of subordination.
2. A challenge to dominant ideologies of meritocracy, colourblindness, race neutrality, objectivity and ahistoricism.
3. A commitment to social justice and the disruption of negative racial relations.
4. Transdisciplinarity that fosters disciplinary cross-pollination and syntheses.
5. The centrality of experiential knowledge and 'voice'.
   (see Bell 1992; Matsuda, Lawrence et al. 1993; Crenshaw, Gotanda et al. 1995; Parker, Deyhle et al. 1999; CCRC 2003; Wing 2003; Lynn 2005; Gillborn 2009; Burdsey 2011; Hylton, Pilkington et al. 2011; Rollock and Gillborn 2011; Delgado 2012; Delgado and Stefancic 2012; Hylton 2015).

Add to this some of the popular CRT critiques of whiteness, interest convergence, microaggressions, intersectionality, critical race feminism and related strands and the theoretical framework of Critical Race Theory reveals itself as a powerful intellectual tool (Delgado and Stefancic 1997; Dixson and Rousseau 2006; Picca and Feagin 2007; Gillborn 2009; Bonilla-Silva 2010; Sue 2010; Hill Collins and Bilge 2016). Like any theoretical framework CRT is subject to misreadings or misinterpretations. Table 1.1 outlines some of the common misapprehensions about some of CRT's core ideas.

TABLE 1.1 Key Critical Race Theory themes

Key CRT themes	Myths and response
1 'Race' and racism are central to any theorising or intervention. Racism is not aberrational or rare – the question is not *do we live in a racist society but we do live in a racist society*.	*Myth* – The concept 'race' is used unproblematically reinforcing racial thinking – It is argued that CRT navigates the landscape of racialised discourses and applies them pragmatically. *Myth* – Other social factors are subordinate to 'race' and racism. CRT does not present a hierarchy of oppressions and seeks to centralise intersecting forms of oppression but without ignoring any racialised dimension, especially where it has been ignored in the past.
2 CRT presents a challenge to dominant ideas of objectivity, meritocracy, colourblindness, race neutrality and equal opportunity.	*Myth* – CRT is a narrow critique of White society CRT is more a series of critiques seeking to positively disrupt and transform racialised power relations regardless of the actors involved. Whiteness (processes) rather than White people (social construct).
3 Social justice and transformation are core goals of CRT.	*Myth* – CRT is targeted solely on an unreasonable and unrealistic agenda for change. CRT is supportive but critical of the liberal incrementalism of the Left. The gains made through the legal system, and state sponsored racial equality are unsatisfactory and slow.
4 Centralise the marginalised voice … naming realities.	*Myth* – CRT is reductionist in nature as it homogenises 'the black experience'. As CRT is anti-essentialist and anti-reductionist CRT is not the domain of any one social group although the experiences of particular groups are so under-theorised the academy is urged to recognise this disparity. They are often 'telling the same stories'.
5 CRT is trans-disciplinary in the spirit of challenging dogma and orthodoxies.	*Myth* – CRT is focused on the law and education only. CRT contributes to our wider understanding of racialised social contexts (and so do other frameworks and perspectives). CRT is necessarily trans-disciplinary and so resists disciplinary strictures and conventions. CRT does not stand in isolation as a theory of the social. And it draws from many disciplines and contexts.

Source: Hylton 2010: 339.

These myths concerning CRT are further considered below.

Myth – The concept 'race' is unproblematically reinforcing racial thinking. It is argued that CRT navigates the landscape of racialised discourses and applies them pragmatically.

Myth – Other social factors are subordinate to 'race' and racism. CRT does not present a hierarchy of oppressions and seeks to centralise intersecting forms of oppression but without ignoring any racialised dimension, especially where it has been ignored in the past.

The centrality of 'race' and racism is significant for critical race scholars because racism is consistently viewed as endemic, systemic, embedded and not an aberration. For many racism in sport is restricted to isolated events, ad hoc occurrences or individual preferences. Patterns of racism are indiscernible to many and defy explanation to most. Yet like the 'miner's canary' (Guinier and Torres 2003) the prevalence of discussions and issues pertaining to 'race' are symptomatic of more odious and toxic problems following close behind. They go so far as to say that the distress of minoritised groups is like the miner's canary as it becomes the first sign of danger for all of us. Sue, Bucceri et al. (2007: 72) add that because newer forms of racism are so difficult to see they *could be likened to carbon monoxide, invisible, but potentially lethal.* They argue this because racism today is more likely to be *aversive,* covert and in opposition to previous years where it tended to be more overt: this 'old fashioned' manifestation has given way to more ambiguous and tenuous experiences (Dovidio 1993; Dovidio and Gaertner 2000).

A CRT approach to 'race' is pragmatic and never unproblematic given the dilemma of its lived reality and its socially constructed nature. However, Critical Race theorists approach race politically while rejecting notions of 'race' neutrality, and critically in terms of a strategic focus on disrupting its real world effects on wellbeing for all (Tate 2016). The costs of racial discrimination and disparities on individuals and communities is well documented in terms of physical and psychological health, family and community, policing, racial profiling and crime, housing and education, and sport is no exception (Feagin and McKinney 2003; Shenglan and Kleiner 2003; Holmes and Smith 2008; Glover 2009; Long, Hylton et al. 2009; Zamudio, Russell et al. 2011; Phillips and Webster 2014; Shipman and Griffiths 2016).

Myth – CRT is a narrow critique of White society. CRT is more a series of critiques seeking to positively disrupt and transform racialised power relations regardless of the actors involved. It considers whiteness (processes) rather than White people (social construct).

Throughout this book a series of critiques emerge on whiteness, colourblindness, meritocracy and approaches to disrupting racism. Examples of critiques that have become important in theorising CRT in social and professional contexts include notions of racial hierarchies and microaggressions (Bell 1992; Sue 2010). Microaggressions are a starting point from which to understand how subtle, aversive forms of racial dynamics can be better framed. As invisible as racism is for many it can be made visible in its most subtle forms by using a framework to explore its variations (Sue, Capodilipo et al. 2007; Sue 2010a; 2010b). By this it is meant that if we can better understand the workings of the environment that we inhabit and the racialised dynamics that are constructed by it then we will also be in a stronger position to upset and alleviate racism's impact in sport.

Amid cries of colourblindness, meritocracy and postraciality in sport, the permanence of racism is emphasised by Bell (1992) and other critical race scholars as a now unremarkable aspect of the world (Hawkins, Carter-Francique et al. 2017). The forms of racism that seem slippery, ambiguous and less visible are the manifestations that are most insidious and requiring of particular clarification in the sporting arena where there is a preoccupation with overt manifestations. A preoccupation with overt racism engenders complacency among institutions, forcing them to be reactive while individual acts, although construed as punishable, buffer the collective from blame. Therefore, the patterns of antiracism in sport tend to reflect a 'firefighting' approach to individual rather than institutional problems.

Microaggressions can be described as everyday communications that negatively impact individuals due to group membership or affiliations. Sue, Capodilipo et al. (2007: 273) define racial microaggressions as,

> Brief and commonplace daily, verbal, behavioural, or environmental indignities, whether intentional or unintentional, that communicate hostile, derogatory, or negative racial slights and insults to the target person or group […] They are not limited to human encounters alone but may also be environmental in nature, as when a person of colour is exposed to an office setting that unintentionally assails his or her racial identity.

Pierce's work in the 1970s has been traced as the first use of the term, where microaggressions were described as *subtle, stunning, often automatic and non-verbal exchanges which are 'put downs'* (Pierce, Carew et al. 1978: cited in Sue 2010: xvi). The cumulative impact of everyday racisms as manifest by microaggressions has been said to cause psychic harm revealed in feelings of reduced self-esteem and wellbeing, and increasing anger and frustration from recognising the slights and seemingly innocuous racialised behaviours on a daily basis. Consequently, Pierce (1970) developed the notion of microaggressions by building on his original concept of 'offensive mechanisms' that manifest innocuously and cumulatively in a microaggressive form rather than more *gross, dramatic, obvious macro-aggressions* [like deliberate violence] (Pierce 1970: 266). For those in sport an understanding of microaggressions is a crucial element in the journey to better understand how racisms are reproduced and for these behaviours to be confronted more effectively.

Microaggressions and blackfacing

At the Australian Open in 2016 some of the fans wore 'blackface' at a Serena Williams tennis match. Blackface is a popular reference to minstrelsy performance that became popular early in the nineteenth century, spawning other names such as 'nxxxxr' minstrelsy (Meer 2005; Pickering 2008; Hylton 2016). Blackface is often reviled for its impersonation of Black people as it draws from the registers of the middle passage, slavery, Black musical forms and stereotypes of the 'negro' (Pickering 2008). Pickering (2008: 3) argued that minstrelsy was particularly infamous for its 'mock blacks and racial mockery', while others such as Meer (2005) suggested that blackface minstrelsy was often used to reinforce the 'benevolence' of slavery, ambiguities of oppression and equivocated over the subordination of Black people. In an era of racially questionable content, British TV's *The Black and White Minstrel Show* was banned in 1978 for its racist content, yet in a range of countries and organisations blackfacing is still an ongoing and controversial issue. For example, Santa's helper 'Black Pete' – *zwarte Piet* – has been described as a racist tradition in the Netherlands; Japanese pop band the Gosperats only perform in blackface and suggest that they mean no harm in their performances so 'get over it'; Brazil's *Zorra* TV show's star, Rodrigo Sant'Anna, was criticised for his caricature blackface character 'Adelaide'; elsewhere, in Colombia there is *son de negro*; in Peru *el negro mama*; and in Spain the tradition of the 'realistic portrayal' of three wise Black men portrayed by blacked-up White men has met with much recent controversy and bans. However, Spanish blackfacing is not restricted to yearly celebrations. F1 driver Lewis Hamilton had a brush with it in 2008 at the Montmelmo circuit in Barcelona as four fans in afros, blackface and T-shirts with the 'Hamilton Family' written on them arrived for 'fun and laughs'. They mingled with other fans who themselves were responsible for racial abuse and insults; the blackface fans denied any wrongdoing on their part (Keeley 2008).

Some argue that face painting at motor racing, tennis and other sport and leisure events is good natured and fun for all. For these people, blackfacing falls into the category of harmless and innocuous fun. However, another reading of it is that no performance of blackface can be neutral in terms of its impact on Black and minoritised ethnic communities. It is undeniable that Black and minoritised communities are sensitive, and therefore vulnerable, to the performance of blackface. Each culture has a general and specific relationship with this manifestation of racial history and in sport it is no different.

In tennis it is commonly viewed that Black players struggle to gain the same level of respect as their White counterparts (Harris and Kyle-DeBose 2007). Serena Williams herself is aware of the racialised history of tennis and the travails of her role models like Althea Gibson and Arthur Ashe, and talks at length of these challenges in relation to her own career; not least the infamous events at Indian Wells where she and her family were racially abused throughout the final that she won in 2001 (Williams 2009). Being told to 'go back to Compton' and 'shouts of nxxxxr!' from a crowd will further sensitise any racialised being to the potential of bigotry in sporting environments (Williams 2009: 71). The Indian Wells final was so traumatic that Williams refused to play in the event for 14 years, happy to risk fines for not competing in this official WTA tour event. In regard to the blackface incident I argue that,

It is unlikely that Serena Williams, whose history of [experiencing] racism is well documented, will see this as anything other than a racial *microaggression*.

The experience of such events for many is harmful and where perpetrators and others try to deny any wrongdoing they invalidate the lived realities of those who experience everyday racism in Australia.

(Hylton 2016)

The microaggressions befalling Serena Williams and Lewis Hamilton could be described as microinsults and microassaults. Microaggressions fall into three categories; (1) microinsults, (2) microassaults, and (3) microinvalidations (Sue 2010). Each can be the result of negative or degrading verbal or non-verbal acts, or affected by environmental issues. The environment of sport can be impacted by broad social, political, economic, cultural, physical, or even ideological concerns. Microinsults are often communicated unintentionally but insensitively in a way that recipients may sense a slight on their racial identity, heritage or background. Microassaults can be unintentional though are more likely to be conscious efforts to racially demean through a verbal or non-verbal attack. Whereas microinvalidations are likely to deny the racialised experiences or history of Black and minoritised ethnic groups.

Consider the team Beitar Jerusalem in Israel and ideas of inclusion, equality, notions of safe space or colourblindness for teams with Arab or Muslim players. Significant hard line sections of the Beitar Jerusalem fans have a history of racism that include targeting and assaulting Palestinian people or protesting to keep 'Beitar pure forever'. After the chairman of the club bought two Muslim players their working environment became more hostile, fans protested goals scored by Muslim players, even the club's trophy room was attacked by arsonists (Sherwood 2013; Dorsey 2016). Beitar was the only club in Israel never to have signed a player from its 20 per cent Arab population (Sherwood 2013) and portrayed the Palestinian–Israeli conflict as *a racial, religious and existentialist conflict rather than a national dispute between two peoples* (Dorsey 2016: 161).

Myth – CRT is targeted solely on an unreasonable and unrealistic agenda for change. CRT is supportive but critical of the liberal incrementalism of the Left. The gains made through the legal system, and state-sponsored racial equality are unsatisfactory and slow.

Linked to the nature and extent of change, the previous assumptions that challenge dominant ideas of objectivity, meritocracy, colourblindness, race neutrality and equal opportunity are crucial in our understanding of how racial inequalities become 'locked in' (Roithmayr 2014). A critique of theories and practices that have accrued limited positive change in relation to racial inequalities have become fundamental targets for activist critical race scholarship. In recent times notions of neoliberalism and postraciality have combined to reinforce the idea that 'race' is no longer relevant, that communal disadvantages such as racial inequalities have dissipated or at least significantly reduced, and that the marketisation of facilities and services will lead to more plural and fair societies (Goldberg 2015).

The myth of meritocracy posits that there is a free and fair pathway to success for all in sport. This is argued in terms of participation, leadership and governance, and in policy domains. The notion of merit is often viewed individualistically, cynically or critically. However, any of these perspectives on merit viewed today and therefore outside of a demonstrably fair and equitable society will often lead to similar inequalities. This idealism denies and invalidates real world experiences of racial inequalities and therefore perpetuates these disparities by leaving current social arrangements undisturbed. A powerful global neoliberalism endorses such individuisation of progress that ignores historical, social and cultural inequalities and discrimination. Adhering to an idealistic meritocracy ideal is a high-risk strategy and one that has been criticised for failing under-served and vulnerable social groups. A cynical view of merit argues that some use these ideas to obfuscate around the seriousness of 'race' and the prevalence of racisms. This approach may concentrate on more traditional and dominative forms of racism. Analogous to this a race-critical lens would support aspirational ideas of meritocracy but with caveats that distance this elusive ideal from thoughts of ignoring racisms, discriminatory behaviours and entrenched power relations.

Aversive racism

Forms of racism in sport such as more aversive practices reinforce the myth of meritocracy through avoidance behaviours that leave racialised policies and practices in place. Aversive racism stymies positive institutional and social change. Where supposed allies of antiracism avoid problems of 'race' it becomes a major constraint because a superficial appearance of support can lead to complacency, over-optimism and a slowing down of progress and institutional commitment to widen diversity and increase participation. Idealists feel vindicated because of symbolic performances of race equality, and cynics are placated as few resources are committed to change (Ahmed 2006; Long and Spracklen 2011). The performance of antiracism rather than the doing of antiracism requires a critical lens to delineate and disrupt racism in sport organisations. Sidestepping 'race' in policy and practice ignores substantive change in institutional arrangements and will continue to reproduce the status quo.

The institutional arrangements in British Olympic legacy promises from 2012 were doomed to failure because the historical institutional racism and racial disparities in British sport were ignored (Hylton and Morpeth 2012; Hylton and Morpeth 2014). This is what Goldberg (2015) describes as a *racial nonracialism* that ignores the structural legacies of past disparities while progressing with agendas that remain ad hoc and piecemeal. Further, few would argue against equal opportunities and yet the minimal practice of redistributive change to favour those historically in need of resources is consistently denied (Delgado and Stefancic 2012). Similarly, a turn to colourblindness, believing that not seeing 'race' is a positive thing (Williams 1997) leads to a form of aversive racism that absolves those most responsible from focusing their resources where racism has had most impact. Both race equality/equal opportunities and colourblindness ideals have led to slow and incremental change, superficial and performative commitments, and act as cloaks for systematic racism to thrive (Matsuda, Lawrence et al. 1993; Hylton 2003; Ahmed 2006; Lusted 2009; Bonilla-Silva 2010; Delgado and Stefancic 2012).

Myth – CRT is reductionist in nature as it homogenises 'the black experience'. As CRT is anti-essentialist and anti-reductionist it is not the domain of any one social group, although the experiences of particular groups are so under-theorised that the academy is urged to recognise this disparity and their experiential similitude. They are often 'telling the same stories' (Delgado and Stefancic 1995). Oppositional discourses sometimes referred to as 'voice', 'giving voice' or 'counter stories' elevate new ideas to supplement what is known or accepted knowledge in the mainstream. Where ideas are shared that are little known, whether through empirical work or experiences revealed for the first time, epistemologies and standpoints may be forced to shift. Earle and Phillips (2013) argue that blackness as an inclusive political term is dated and redolent of a time in the context of the major colonial diasporic shifts to the UK over the 1960s, 1970s and 1980s. A positive identification with blackness meant a direct resistance to the overtly fascistic tendencies of established White groups, while globally the American Civil Rights Movement and South Africa's battle with apartheid meant that a collective Black identity engendered a feeling of liberation and resistance from White oppressors through a collective struggle. Yet embedded in this political project lies the danger of a conflation of struggles and the homogenisation of identities and experiences. Given these caveats, the Black[1] experience is clearly a unifying political term rather than a descriptive homogenising one. The 'Black experience' becomes a starting point for a decolonising narrative of a diversity of ideas that can support and challenge mainstream knowledge. What is reductionist and anti-intellectual is the exclusion of marginalised people and ideas as a result of a 'master' narrative (Leonardo 2005; Zamudio, Russell et al. 2011; Delgado 2012).

Though Black and minoritised ethnic people have oppression in common, their forms delineate at the point of their intersections with 'race'. Though large groups with a shared oppression may have more political power, the specifics of intersectionality can offer a more nuanced understanding of 'race' and racism in sport and society today. Elsewhere I argue that,

> The anti-essentialism of the intersectionality thesis strengthens a CRT framework especially as the CRT emphasis on centring 'race' can be misconstrued as essentialism. Intersectionality is one of the mechanisms used in CRT to emphasise that though the starting point for CRT is 'race' and racism there is no intention to lose sight of the complexities of the intersection of 'race' with the constructed and identity related nature of other forms of oppression.
>
> *(Hylton 2012: 29)*

Just as the notion of 'voice' does not embrace one singular, essential idea, intersectionality enables CRT to more convincingly analyse these complexities further (Dixson and Rousseau 2005). For example, Hill Collins and Bilge (2016) emphasise that identities affect each other in mutually constructing ways and these power relations gain meaning from each other accordingly. So intersectionality is more than the analysis of intersecting forms of oppression, but also a dynamic critique of these intersections *across domains of power, namely structural, disciplinary, cultural and personal* (Hill Collins and Bilge 2016: 27).

Myth – CRT is focused on the law and education only. CRT contributes to our wider understanding of racialised social contexts [and so do other frameworks and perspectives] – CRT is necessarily trans-disciplinary and so resists disciplinary strictures and conventions. CRT does not stand in isolation as a theory of the social. And it draws from multiple disciplines and contexts.

In 2011 a significant collection of work was bound into the British-based book *Atlantic Crossings* that was the result of the first major conference on CRT in the UK (Hylton, Pilkington et al. 2011). Contributors acknowledged the contribution of CRT from North America while establishing its resonance and applicability in the UK, Europe and beyond. Within this collection there were contributions on education, class, whiteness, sport, mixed race studies, gender and intersectionality, and the media. It was the first time that a particular type of CRT was emphasised as 'BritCrit' yet it only hinted at the trans-disciplinary nature of CRT and the way it eschews the dogma that plagues some perspectives with a poverty of ideas. CRT is now found in a wide range of disciplines not limited to but including gender and 'race'/critical feminism (Wing 2003; Childers-McKee and Hytten 2015), entrepreneurship (Gold 2016), public health (Ford and Airhihenbuwa 2010), indigeneity (McKinley and Brayboy 2006; Schuloff 2015), sport and PE (Harrison, Azzarito et al. 2004; Burdsey 2011; Agyemang and Singer 2014), psychology (Salter and Adams 2013), disability studies (Annamma, Connor et al. 2013; Dávila 2015), criminology (Warde 2012; Glynn 2014), religious studies (Tranby and Hartmann 2008; Boutros 2015), research methods (Parker, Deyhle et al. 1999), arts and the media (Cummings 2010; Aleman and Aleman 2016) to name a few.

Critical 'race' practice – Critical Race Theory

In a study of four major local authorities in England I examined the prevalence of 'race' consciousness and levels of colourblindness in sport policy implementation. Using a Critical Race Theory framework 'race' and (anti)racism, racial equality and social transformation were central to the initial questions being asked of three large local authority case studies in the north of England (Hylton 2003). Giddens' (1984) notion of duality of structure alerts us to the nature of organisations being constituted of individuals ... they are the organisation. Conversely organisations are constitutive of individuals as the actions of actors are influenced by the customs, policies and practices of their employer. These are simple factors often missed in the analyses of why organisations struggle to include a diversity of employees and/ or participants in their sport. In exploring these dynamics, the key areas that I applied a CRT lens to were as follows:

1.   I examined the colourblind, 'race'-neutral meritocracy, and racism in local government sport by first examining local authority policymakers and

practitioners and the ideologies that underpinned their policy decisions. I examined 'critical moments' in each organisation where the integrity of their adherence to race equality was being tested. These 'critical moments' were recorded by documenting how race equality stood up to the 'real world' pressures of change in these large municipal organisations. Opinions, attitudes and ideologies established the assumptive world of each senior practitioner and policymaker during the course of this research.

2. Second, the study tested the dominant views of each institution (the 'system') (Ouseley 1990) by privileging the Black voice 'counter story' through incorporating an ethnography of a Black sport pressure group. In addition to the original methodology, the study was able to explore the experience and status of Black people in municipal sport and explore their need for political mobilisation.

3. Third, the study was able to challenge conventional methodologies through its use of a 'counter narrative' from the configuration of research tools, the centralising of 'race', and racism as normal, in addition to the actual findings from the field. The CRT perspective and counter narrative offered a 'plurivocality' (new/many voices) for the academy to hear. The ontological standpoint of the study and its implications for the academic and political community challenged some of the complacency and assumptions implicit within the key themes in sport, leisure and policy studies literature; thus challenging those on the Left as well as the Right.

4. And finally, social change and transformation was the focus of the study because without it, and its connection with theory and practice, it would not have been a suitable project for CRT.

(Long, Hylton et al. 2000; Spracklen, Hylton et al. 2006; Hylton 2009).

Sport and racial standing

One of the most intriguing ideas that has emerged from CRT is Derrick Bell's Rules of Racial Standing that critically illustrates the ambiguous and strategic nature of racism. Bell's five rules are outlined here in relation to recent controversies in sport. Bell's first rule outlines how Black people are often denied standing when they discuss their negative experiences of racism. Bell, a notable figure in CRT, utilised the notion of 'denied standing' to denote how suspicion follows Black people about their motives where matters of 'race' and racism are concerned. Many will have experienced getting a puzzling reception when speaking with folks about their, or other peoples' experiences of 'race' and racism. Black people's struggle to have their complex, lived, racialised experiences heard, believed and acted upon is one famously told by White journalist John Howard Griffin in 1959. Howard Griffin saw himself as an expert in issues of 'race' yet felt he knew little of the African Americans he lived with side by side. Further, in his explanation to the international *Negro* [sic] magazine editor who financed his work he said, the best way to find out *if* we had second-class citizens and what their plight was would be *to become one of them.*

(Howard Griffin 2010: 3)

Howard Griffin saw no irony in his position in a racial hierarchy that reinforced how knowledge of the racialised other was formed. His vagueness on the question of racism in the US at that time hints at the epistemologies of ignorance that Sullivan and Tuana (2007) argue ruling classes can draw upon to deny their complicity in reinforcing racial inequalities. However, while embarking upon this project Howard Griffin exemplified the implicit lack of confidence shown in Black people to authoritatively expound on the dynamics of 'race', and in the credibility of their claims of indignities, humiliation and discrimination.

Internationally and across sports there are many examples of sportsmen and women whose claims of racialised discrimination have been ignored or requiring of influential others for them to be taken seriously. Bell (1992) argued that often claims of racism are viewed as exaggerated, fabricated, invalid and therefore seen as 'special pleading'. Notable examples have been witnessed recently in tennis, Formula 1 racing, football, basketball, and even golf. In 2013 the Indigenous Australian, Adam Goodes, found himself on the pitch and having to defend himself from racial abuse in the stands as an Australian Football League (AFL) player. Goodes pointed out the instigator 20 years after a similar iconic incident with St. Kilda's Nicky Winmar who raised his shirt and finger, pointing to his black skin as he shouted to racists in the Collingwood crowd that *I'm black and I'm proud to be black* (Klugman and Osmond 2013: 5). Yet, long-term public consciousness in Australia is susceptible to slippage within and across generations as Goodes' perpetrator was 13 years old. She called him *An Ape!* (Huxley 2015). Not only that, Goodes received constant barracking throughout the game for his principled and spirited response. If that were not all, the girl's mother, with support from others including media representatives, called upon Goodes to apologise for his actions that led to the girl being ejected from the stadium.

Coram and Hallinan (2017) reject what they see as these justifications of racism in Australia, as reflected in the case of Adam Goodes. The constant booing of Goodes in Australian stadia has signatures of racial vilification, while establishing the conditions for arguments that deny racism in everyday crowd behaviours. The defence to accusations of racism that the booing of one Indigenous player and not all cannot equate to racism, denies Goodes and other Indigenous players' history of having to resist racism (Coram and Hallinan 2017: 101). The operation of narrow definitions of racism as the domain of a few isolated individuals ignores more pernicious structural damaging forms. Ignoring them leads to everyday microaggressions and the reifying of sporting arenas as hostile to those with particular identities. Ignoring the experiences of the racialised other and the denial of intent bears the hallmark of contemporary racism in sport. Goodes was accused of 'picking on', 'targetting' and 'singling out' a vulnerable child while he was urged to 'stop carrying on', 'accept the taunts' and 'man up' (Huxley 2015).

There have been numerous acts of resistance to racism in sport that have invariably drawn approbrium from sections of society. In addition to Winmar and Goodes, such acts of resistance by Black sportspeople have taken time to gain traction because there has not been enough recognition from those not traditionally impacted by racism in society. Other acts of resistance reduced to 'special pleading' include Muhammad Ali's rejection of the Vietnam War draft to highlight racism in the US; and the Olympic Project for Human Rights, established to broaden the ethnic diversity in sport in predominantly White institutions that led to Tommie Smith and John Carlos' fists raised to the Mexico sky at the 1968 Olympic Games before being ejected from the Games (Marqusee 1995). This chain of events continued in 2015 in Missouri where the Missouri College football team refused to play until the administration responded to the multiple racisms on campus. Similarly, in 2016 the San Francisco 49ers player Colin Kaepernick's refusal to stand for the US national anthem to protest police brutality in America has divided opinion (Nadkarni 2015; Krasovic 2016).

What each of these examples have in common is Rule 1 of the Rules of Racial Standing that argues there is a lack of consensus on the efficacy of the claims by victims of racism by those in power. The accusation of 'special pleading' firmly covers each of these circumstances while it draws attention to (a) how racism is defended in sport and society, (b) the everyday nature of racism, and (c) how alienation and invalidation lead to forced points of resistance in and through sport. Rule 2 explains this phenomenon further by outlining that Black witnesses to racism are less effective than those implicated in reinforcing racism. This precarious position was not articulated by John Howard Griffin but he intuitively knew that African Americans had *diminished standing* and that his position of power in what Bell (1992: 112) described as 'the oppressor class' enabled him to make claims with more gravitas than renowned Black scholars of the era such as Fanon (1967), Du Bois (1994; 1998) and Ellison (1965).

In sport, ex-Arsenal and England player and association football commentator Ian Wright acknowledged the asymmetrical power relations of the Black player versus those more representative of the dominant hegemony of football's hierarchy. Wright's response on CNN (2013) about Kevin Prince Boateng's 'walk-off' the pitch while being victimised by Pro Patria racists in the stadium caused him to reflect on his own denied standing (RRS1) during his distinguished playing career and the relatively diminished standing (RRS2) of Black players whose sole actions are not enough to force cultures in sport to make the necessary attitudinal and policy changes against racism. Wright went on to state,

> As a Black player, being racially abused, people will listen to you but they'll say 'ahh look at him playing the race card' … I had to deal with that all my life, but if you have the top White players alongside you, like with Prince Boateng when they walked off with him … that's fine. But if you walk off as a black guy people will say he's got a chip on his shoulder, he's walked off and doesn't care about his team.

> *(CNN 2013)*

Bell argues that depending upon the position that Black people take on race in or against influential institutions, they can be privileged with standing commensurate with their benefit to those with most power or influence.

Black people are less likely to have diminished racial standing where they criticise others acting to disparage/upset powerful elites. In many ways these actors are likely to receive *enhanced standing* (RRS3) as in the case of ex-Chelsea and England player Ashley Cole.

Cole was one of the first players to state 'I didn't hear John Terry make any racist comments' (Irwin 2011). Terry had been found guilty by the English Football Association of breaching their rules by using racially abusive language against West Ham player Anton Ferdinand. Cole's evidence was key in presenting enough doubt for an acquittal at Westminster Magistrates Court. The media were also quick to present Cole's views, as the Terry defence was built upon it. Cole's ethnicity has been described as 'Black mixed heritage' (Christian 2011). Cole's blackness was used skilfully by then England captain Terry, the media and others who in this case privileged the voice of a Black sportsperson in a case of racism. In this case of racism, the White captain of England and Chelsea endorsed a Black face who was voluntarily contradicting accusations of White racism. The institution of football mobilised its defence, which included media sources like the *Sun* and the *Telegraph*, multiple unsolicited validations of John Terry's character, and importantly this high-profile international Black professional. Presumably, Cole's opposition to other Black views was enhanced by those in defence of this establishment figure. As someone who seemingly understands the finer manifestations of racism in this case, Cole added gravitas to the claims that England captain John Terry was not racist.

The fourth Rule of Racial Standing was explained by Bell (1992: 117) as,

> When a black person or a group makes a statement or takes an action that the white community or vocal components thereof deem 'outrageous', the latter will actively recruit blacks willing to refute the statement or condemn the action. Blacks who respond to the call for condemnation will receive superstanding status.

This can be illustrated in the example of Jessie Owens who was elevated to *superstanding* as an envoy of the US Olympic Committee and the IOC to speak against Black protesters from the Olympic Project for Human Rights (OPHR). OPHR members included Tommie Smith and John Carlos, who were leading calls for the IOC and the US Olympic Committee to increase the representation of Black people in athletics as performers and leaders, and for them to be more proactive in challenging racism in the sport. Owens' superstanding shifted him from being a man suspended as an amateur by Avery Brundage after the 1936 Olympics which reduced him to competing in novelty competitions such as racing against horses for money, to an African American man willing to change his status in the eyes of such powerful establishment figures by publicly speaking out against Smith, Carlos and other such projects.

Bell (1992: 123) argues that a burden of blackness is a need for racial awareness and that any criticism of other people in matters of 'race' is not always equitable. The threat of enhanced or superstanding must be considered not just in the light of controversial issues but more importantly in more everyday ones that might do the work of reinforcing and perpetuating racial hierarchies in the most subtle of ways. For example, in a period where racism against Black players was spiking, a different application of superstanding from Bell's fourth rule was illustrated by ex-Celtic and West Ham player Paulo Di Canio, who used his Black 'friends' to defend his position as a self-proclaimed fascist after pictures of him playing for Lazio in Italy showed him using a Nazi salute. In response to this he replied 'I am a fascist, not a racist!' (Duff 2005). More significantly the superstanding that he attributed to his Black professional colleagues was a transparent strategy to elevate the opinion of the public in his favour. He argued that,

> The people who know me can change that idea quickly. When I was in England my best friends were Trevor Sinclair and Chris Powell, the Charlton manager – they can tell you everything about my character.
>
> *(Agencies 2013)*

Trevor Sinclair and Chris Powell are highly respected ex-professional players. Their role for Di Canio was to show the media that because they were team mates and are Black they could vouch for his claims of not being a racist fascist. Though the distinction of being a fascist versus being a racist fascist was lost on most people, Di Canio repeatedly refused to point out the difference. In this case the privileging of the Black voice on issues of racism to defend a high-profile figure reaped little success as Sinclair described Di Canio as 'Mad as a hatter' (Association 2013) while Powell said, 'You'll have to ask him' (Guardian 2013).

For Bell (1992: 124), the cost of understanding how the first four Rules of Racial Standing work is the recognition that these issues will recursively manifest time and again. The more one becomes sensitised to the way racial dynamics work is to recognise their systemic and embedded nature. He goes on to state that,

> Using this knowledge, one gains the gift of prophecy about racism, its essence, its goals, even its remedies. The price of this knowledge is the frustration that follows recognition that no amount of public prophecy, no matter its accuracy, can either repeal the Rules of Racial Standing or prevent their operation.

The fifth Rule of Racial Standing shakes any complacency from claims that 'race' and racism are inconsequential, ad hoc or the domain of bigoted individuals. Such ideas endorse views that racism in society is far more serious and challenging a problem than some might suggest: structural, multifaceted, ambiguous, accidental and deliberate, conscious and unconscious, personal, cultural and structural, all at the same time. Racism is a complex interconnection of racialised actions and processes that unfairly impact individuals and groups because of their racial and/or minoritised background.

Introduction to the chapters

The claim that the veil will continue indefinitely is an assertion by Winant (2004: 34), who saw issues of racial identity, the doggedness of racism and its injustices, and the precarious state of racial democracy as *three patterns to be woven into the fabric of the veil* (Du Bois 1994; 1998). The following chapters build upon these ideas by exploring and explaining the way 'race' and racism appear institutionally, structure identities, lead to modes of resistance, and affect society in real and virtual spaces.

Chapter 2 examines 'race', sport coaching and leadership to focus debates on the general under-representation of Black leaders in sport. It examines issues of diversity by drawing on a multilevel analysis (Cunningham 2010) that centres debates on unconscious bias, aversive racism (Kovel 1970; Gaertner and Dovidio 2005) and prototypes of leadership (Logan 2011). Governance is also an issue in this chapter, where whiteness in sport is conspicuous and easily propagated (Proxmire 2008; Sporting Equals 2016). The chapter draws on examples from studies on 'race', sport coaching and leadership to emphasise the challenges faced by national governing bodies and national governing organisations of sport (Fletcher, Piggot et al. 2014; Norman, North et al. 2014; Hylton and Rankin 2016).

Chapter 3 examines whiteness as concept, identity and process in sport and leisure research. In particular, it engenders a conversation with research-active scholars to reveal how individual identities impact upon how research is conducted and how racialised power is resisted, reinforced and created. While White male power dominates the academy, their voices are invited here to reflect upon research on 'race' mainly because these critically reflective voices are inconsistently directly critiqued. Where authors like Gallagher (2000) found the supremacy of whiteness and White identities as conscious structurating factors, White academics are invited to speak of such issues in their approach to conducting meaningful critical work in sport and leisure (Razack 1999; Fine 2004; Blaisdell 2009; Gillborn 2011; Roithmayr 2014).

Chapter 4 unpacks how Brohm (1989), in describing sport as *a prison of measured time*, was taking as his cue the instrumental and mythopoetic elements of sport-related activity in society. In a prison, sport can be used as a way to represent self, a technical means to an end, a symbolic depiction of productivity, a site of diversion and transmitter of ideological values. Social control, escapism and catharsis emerge as relatively predictable themes given the literature on the benefits of sport. This chapter explores the significance of 'race' in the way prisoners engage in sport and recreation. To explore some of these issues, the chapter draws on a study conducted in a prison in the north of England with a view to understanding what sport means for prisoners and what import 'race' may have for them. The prisoners' use of sport becomes one of the factors that contributes to establishing a routine. It also becomes a factor that is imbued with meaning and potential physical, psychological and social benefits, not so well researched in the prison and sport literature. The implications for practice are manifold in regards to the prison service having a much clearer grounding of the personal and environmental drivers of participation in sport, its various settings and social outcomes. To understand these processes and practices is to begin to reduce the potential for ineffective practice, and facilitating wellbeing through enabling those characteristics of sport and physical activity that prisoners recognise as productive, positive and worthwhile.

Chapter 5 explores how 'race' and racism are manifest and played out online in what has been argued to be an egalitarian, 'post-race' space. It considers how those online may feel less accountable to social norms and mores as they do when offline. Online their anonymous identities and online protocols blur notions of authenticity and acceptability in racialised debates. Hall (1998) holds the position that modernist ideas of traditional processes of building arguments and opinion with others, rehearsing ideas, and developing consensus before publication are less relevant on the internet. As a consequence, the potential for extremism, bigotry, and the perpetuation of racialised ideologies are more likely to be openly expressed.

The chapter examines online dispositions to issues of 'race' and racism. It is based upon analysis from findings of blog responses to an article on the acrimonious racialised split between Tiger Woods and his caddie in 2011. The analysis is of seventy anonymous Yahoo! Blog responses. The responses reflect a range of contradictory perspectives that draw on racialised discourses less prevalent in offline debates where actors are likely to be more circumspect. These ambiguous online identities are identifiable only through arbitrary user names and, without socio-biographic attributes that could help to locate them, make a reading of 'race' and racism in cyberspace even more complicated than offline. Notwithstanding these unavoidable challenges, the chapter analyses the dispositions and politics portrayed by online respondents to racism in sport and considers the methodological, political and philosophical issues of understanding the outcomes of racialised thinking or 'racial mechanics' (Kang 2003).

Chapter 6 interrogates reverse discourse (Weaver 2010) to explore how language is used as a device for resistance in sport. Within this, the chapter examines how humour is applied as a coping strategy. Humour has been described as a form of catharsis, community building, educational, protection, and technique of anti-oppression in the sharing of racialised stories (Bowers 2005; Gaggiano 2005; Weaver 2010; Weaver 2011). The study explores how processes of 'reverse humour' work to dissipate the impact of negative experiences of racism. The chapter is based upon narrative data from Black (BME) football coaches. Through the sharing of their experiences in sport, and at leisure, to 'open a window onto ignored or alternative realities', 'counter-storytelling' techniques through humour are examined.

Chapter 7 considers the major debates from each of the chapters and teases out the utility of a Critical Race Theory framework for examining racialised problematics in sport and leisure. This final chapter centres on an examination of the place of 'race' and its intersections, and racism in areas of sport that many would overlook. Historically this has led to such issues being under-researched and under-theorised. Regardless of the topic, a CRT critique on for example ice skating, tennis, swimming, governance, college sports, humour, gendered racism, basketball, whiteness, motor racing, the seaside or even cycling can take ordinary phenomena and make them extraordinary, revealing how everyday realities from the living room to the boardroom are replete with signatures of injustice and the potential for resistance and change. As structural racisms and patriarchy tessellate with institutional and micro levels, microaggressions, aversive and unconscious/implicit bias, whiteness and White supremacy do the everyday work of maintaining 'race' talk, power relations and the status quo.

Note

1   Unifying political terms differ over space and time. 'Black' is not always the unifying term in some domains. For example, 'people of colour' is a term used quite commonly as a unifying political concept in North American circles while in others indigeneity is the source of these identities.

2

'RACE', SPORT COACHING AND LEADERSHIP

> And to this day, even in sports where they have dominated as athletes, one finds the
> number of blacks in both the front office and on-the-field leadership in decision
> making and authority positions to be either disproportionately low or non-existent.
>
> *Harry Edwards (1979: 117)*

For many in sport, the structural nature of racism in society means there is no
surprise that these introductory words of scholar and activist Harry Edwards, still
ring true. If 'race' is a fundamental fault line in our society then so must it structure
our sport coaching and leadership domains. Edwards still speaks truth to the institution of sport almost 40 years after he made this statement. Given the amount of
global interest in 'race' and issues of diversity in society, many presume that sport
leadership arenas are the least troubled in regard to achieving the aspirational social
goals of diversity, equity and inclusion (Cunningham 2010; Long and Spracklen
2011). Where we accept the structural nature of racism in society we should also
consider the role of sport coaching and leadership structures as implicated within.
We must then turn a weather eye to not only explore the nature and extent of
racism in sport coaching and its administration but also the nature of the insidious
racial dynamics. A clearer view of 'race' problematics in sport will share the concerns of Harry Edwards with those in the field who are less critical of them. This
chapter can also contribute to the warnings of Ospina and Foldy (2009), who also
emphasise the persistent relevance of 'race' in leadership contexts, describing 'race'
as playing a significant part in the way lives are structured and lived.

This chapter examines 'race', sport coaching and leadership to focus debates on
the general under-representation of Black leaders in sport. It examines issues of
diversity by drawing on a multilevel analysis (Cunningham 2010) that centres
debates on unconscious bias, aversive racism (Kovel 1970; Gaertner and Dovidio
2005) and prototypes of leadership (Logan 2011). Governance is also an issue in

this chapter where whiteness in sport is shown to be conspicuous and easily propagated (Proxmire 2008; Sporting Equals 2016). Later in the chapter examples from studies on 'race', sport coaching and leadership emphasise the challenges faced by national governing bodies and national governing organisations (Fletcher, Piggot et al. 2014; Norman, North et al. 2014; Hylton and Rankin 2016).

'Race' has become a significant factor considered to directly and indirectly affect the way we experience sport as spectators, players and officials. Sport is unsurprisingly a pastime which for a small and fortunate minority is a vehicle for social mobility and in other cases significant racial exclusions. It is a commonly held view that sport is a meritocracy that continues to work to find and promote the best leaders from the grassroots to the highest offices. However, a perennial contradiction in this regard remains the paucity of Black leaders and coaches making their way through the player pipeline to become the next generation of coaches, leaders and senior administrators. Though the debate ensues there persists a desperation without inspiration from key stakeholders in sport to consistently engage with these ongoing issues. Ospina and Foldy (2009: 876) conclude that

> If society, communities and individuals are significantly informed by race, then leadership must be as well.

However, it is no secret that in some sports, even when Black managers or leaders have been qualified with the necessary experience, they have still been overlooked for interviews in professional sport environments. This hints at the complexity of racial dynamics as individual and institutional manifestations lead to a variety of incomprehensible outcomes. It has become a mantra for some in sport that the best people will always get the job, even though it seems that stereotypes of intellect and physicality constrain opportunities for Black players on leadership pathways. In some sports, action is being taken to manage the perpetual racialised disparities in the player–leader pipeline. Baseball, American football (NFL) and association football (soccer) have taken a variety of steps to acknowledge the way their sports have developed: paradoxically while marginalising players often lauded and loved on the playing field as their qualities off the field are regularly ignored (see Table 2.1).

The player–leader pipeline has become a cause for concern for many. Even the diversity of governing bodies has been brought to the attention of key funding agents reluctantly applying a punitive 'stick' to an issue where carrots have not worked (Sporting Equals 2016). Sporting Equals'[1] study of the ethnic breakdown of national governing bodies demonstrates the stark realities of these disparities where Black, Asian and minority ethnic populations boast 14 per cent of the population in the UK (see Tables 2.2 and 2.3).

As Table 2.1, Table 2.2 hints at the lack of diversity in governance across sixty-eight major sporting organisations in the UK. This is further exacerbated by the lack of diversity of national governing body members as shown in Table 2.3. According to Bridgewater (2014) only 4.4 per cent of Black and minoritised ethnic footballers have taken on the role of coaches, managers or related roles since 1992.

TABLE 2.1 Percentage of minorities in key roles at the start of 2008 season

	Major League Baseball	National Basketball Association	National Football League
Players	40.1%	80%	69%
Managers/head coaches	27%	40%	19%
Coaches/assistant coaches	31%	42%	38%
CEOs	0%	23%	0%
General managers	6%	23%	13%
Vice presidents	10%	15%	8%

Source: Reproduced by kind permission of Douglas C. Proxmire (Proxmire 2008: 8).

TABLE 2.2 National governing body chairs and CEOs

No. national governing bodies	No. Black, Asian and minority ethnic chairs	No. Black, Asian and minority ethnic CEOs
68	1	1

Source: Data taken from Sporting Equals (2016: 2).

TABLE 2.3 National governing body members (ethnicity)

No. national governing body members	No. Black, Asian and minority ethnic members
601	26 (4%)

Source: Data taken from Sporting Equals (2016: 2).

In this time, 25 per cent of all footballers have been Black and minority ethnic (Bridgewater, 2014). Stereotyping, institutional racism, prototypes of effective managers and narrow conceptions of effective leadership reproduce the ideologies of those who can and cannot lead at the highest levels. Coupled with recruitment processes and networks that lack transparency, racial and gendered outcomes lead to a lack of diversity in the sporting workplace (Duru 2011).

Such statistics reveal the highest levels of the sporting landscape racialised as White in the UK, yet a similar story of diversity is replicated in particular where 'race', gender and their intersections are in question. Though the appearance of 'race' may not offer a fully informed picture of self-described identities, what we do see is the privileging of whiteness and White leader prototypes that Logan (2011: 447) argues maintains a racialised leadership terrain by reproducing White people as leaders.

A multilevel approach to 'race' and sport leadership

A multilevel overview of the dynamics of 'race', sport coaching and leadership that acknowledges the influences of the external environment, institutional processes and culture, and individual level behaviours assists a critical analysis of racial dynamics in sport. Analyses that explicate these connections in sport coaching and leadership domains may offer a practical frame to explain why racialised behaviours occur, how they are maintained, and more importantly how they might be resisted. A multilevel analysis which incorporates a frame that takes into account macro-, meso- and micro-level critiques is useful to identify contested sites in sport that enable focused examinations of specific problems. This ensures a move beyond the important broad discussion of issues in sport to a point of making complex processes and practices visible so as to disrupt them. For instance, Cunningham (2010) describes a multilevel model as one that explores (1) macro factors such as institutionalised practices and political climate, (2) meso factors such as prejudice on the part of decision makers, leadership prototypes and organisational culture of diversity, and (3) micro factors such as coaching expectations and intentions, and occupational turnover.

Cunningham's (2010) use of the term 'macro' also relates to external forces beyond organisations. For example, the prevalence and embeddedness of structural racisms in society leading to structurating, institutionalised practices within organisations. The broader cultural, political and economic conditions across each nation state and globally in the case of high-level sports directly impact the internal environment of sport(s). Racism in sport is not an insignificant matter, yet sport is part of a recursive process of call and response where behaviours and practices within and without its control are manifest, reconstructed, perpetuated and resisted within. Sport is a significant cultural tool, and because it is constituted and constitutive of society, it is not devoid of responsibility in the struggle against racism. Further, Burton and Leberman (2015) emphasise how institutional practice can contribute to reinforcing biases toward particular forms of leaders which can be further augmented by policies that exaggerate these behaviours.

Critical Race Theory was initially developed as a foil to disrupt racialised inequalities in the law and elsewhere (Crenshaw, Gotanda et al. 1995). More specifically, CRT emerged out of the critical legal studies dissatisfaction with the inequities woven into the fabric of the law and legal governance (Delgado 2012). It was symptomatic of the broader political and legal environment that ensured a state-sponsored racism that endorsed notions of neutrality, objectivity and colour-blindness to obscure how 'race' structures our experiences from kindergarten to retirement. Our work and play are inextricably linked with the influence of state inequities often incorporated into approaches to equal opportunities legislation and what is/is not acceptable across facilities and services in the public domain. In sport, basic employment practices and the location of approaches to diversity are framed in equalities legislation, and national and international rules and codes. When these institutional and/or statutory policies are under-developed, ambiguous, or lack commitment to transforming social arrangements, history has shown that other priorities will be promoted in their stead by organisations (Ahmed 2006; Long and Spracklen 2011).

Meso-level factors focus analyses that consider internal organisational cultures in regard to the way sport structures, customs and practices result in racialised inequalities. Organisations that regularly under-perform in the diversity of their leadership and governance structures will often have developed a culture that reproduces this environment through hiring practices, networks and the internal environment that it engenders. Cunningham (2010) emphasises that meso analyses on 'race' and sport that might explain the under-representation of leaders and coaches tend to draw on the role of prejudice and discrimination in this process. On this matter, he argues that,

> Prejudice is a psychological term focusing on people's attitudes and beliefs while discrimination has sociological foundations and is concerned with people's behaviours. Both prejudice and discrimination are multi-dimensional constructs.
>
> *(Cunningham 2010: 399)*

This distinction is pertinent in the discussion of 'race', sport coaching and leadership in the way we frame specific problems. For example, unconscious bias is often used as a reason for the lack of diversity in sport organisations, yet unconscious bias is purely a state of mind, a form of prejudice that *leads to* active discrimination. Discrimination involves *implementing* forms of bias and prejudice, consciously or unconsciously, or individually or institutionally in a way that disadvantages others from particular social backgrounds. Further, discrimination in itself has been evidenced to impact access or the way people are treated in organisations which, individually or in concert with a range of other unconscionable experiences, can trigger (self) exclusions from networks, jobs and professions. An organisational culture reinforces hegemonic normative dispositions that establish the dominant attitudes and ideologies underpinning everyday assumptions and behaviours (Hylton 2003; Hylton and Rankin 2016). Workplaces and sporting arenas can mirror such attitudes and opinions to the point that they become engrained and invisible to key stakeholders. Workplace culture as reflected by bias, discrimination and racial disparities become inextricably linked to everyday business, thus making resistance to change a task requiring real commitment, critical insight and diplomacy.

On a *micro* level, many factors affect the decisions made about coaching and leadership in sport environments. If individuals are treated differently or perceive that they or people like them are treated unfavourably then they will act to assimilate, accommodate, or resist. To assimilate is to acquiesce to the organisational culture and to take on dominant modes of thinking and behaving in regards to the relative merits of race equality and diversity. This may be positive or negative, though it generally comes at a personal cost for those affected in under-performing organisations that lack diversity or poorly conceive of the significance of 'race' and its intersections. Similarly, accommodating dominant forms of working may come with a higher personal cost *because of* the conscious acceptance of ways of working that are anathema to the individual's politics or professional disposition. However, the highest risk position for an individual is one that acts in opposition to the way institutions behave in relation to 'race'; a position that resists and struggles against the everyday biases and racialised working of sport. The personal and professional costs of resistance to institutional norms has the potential to be the most rewarding or the most psychologically damaging. These leaders and coaches may also suffer because of a lack of access to networks, and unfavourable treatment, in their ability to generate the social capital to progress through the system; human capital in reduced opportunities for job training, experience and educational advancement; and cultural capital to learn effective behaviours, and discourses valued by ingroups that would facilitate progression (Burton and Leberman 2015). In any case, an emotional burden is placed upon the marginalised leader. Individuals make personal and professional decisions based on their experience of engagement at multiple levels of sport and so consideration of these challenges in regards to 'race' and leadership requires a comprehensive critique of the appropriateness, rigour and robustness of their interventions as a foil to context-, institution- and sector-specific issues.

Intersectional issues

Ospina and Foldy (2009) reveal four key issues in relation to 'race' and ethnicity in leadership that emerge contrary to the relative success of Black people in many domains of sport and society. (1) 'Race' is an everyday concern or fault line, (2) where leadership is researched, context is rarely addressed, (3) diversity in the workforce is under-valued and misunderstood, and (4) a focus on 'race' helps to explain the place of institutionalised power in perpetuating inequalities and privileges. Within this context, women are under-represented in leadership and coaching, and Black women are even further behind in this regard (Norman 2010; Carter-Francique, Lawrence et al. 2011). To complicate matters, diversity in sport management has a tendency to emphasise the experiences of Black men in regard to 'race' and White women where gender is concerned, thus emphasising the relative novelty of the lived experiences of Black women (Jean and Feagin 1998; Scraton 2001; Borland and Bruening 2010; Bruno Massao and Fasting 2014). We know very little of what has been described as a *double burden*, the way 'race' *and* gender play out in sport (Jean and Feagin 1998). This oversight in the literature is reflected at all levels and thus produces skewed representations of marginalisation where intersections of 'race', gender and class are considered separately (Bruno Massao and Fasting 2014). Explanations for this include the paucity of Black women as leaders in sport, their absence as knowledge formers in the academy, their marginality in studies of 'race', gender and identities, and their relative absence as the subjects of knowledge through their shared experience. This also speaks to the under-utilised work of Black feminism and the peripheral application of intersectionality in sport and leisure theorising. Mowatt, French et al. (2013) and Mirza (2006) argue that contradictions depict the perception of Black women as their *hypervisibility* as stereotyped bodies is juxtaposed with their *invisibility* in the academy, in research, and in certain roles and spaces. Invisibility in the academy means few challenges to the hypervisibility of disempowering stereotypes that range from the 'angry black woman', nurturing subordinate images, and hyper-sexualised representations (Carter-Francique, Lawrence et al. 2011). Mowatt, French et al. (2013: 647) argue that,

> If leisure studies is to expand theory and research to explore Black women's realities, prioritizing knowledge by Black women themselves, and adopting a theoretical framework to contextualise these realities becomes particularly paramount.

In regards to the trope of the 'angry black woman', Mowatt, French et al. (2013: 652) state that Black women often face racism, sexism and cultural insensitivity. They argue that, when they voice their opinions about issues, they are labelled as troublemakers, and the fact that these are core traits of a leadership position in sport presents a serious problem for Black women. Mowatt, French et al. (2013), outline how Black professionals find their work being devalued, especially where there is a focus on 'race', ethnicity and diversity. The notion of feeling 'overexposed' in regard to these issues emerged through their experiencing of microaggressions (Sue 2010; Burdsey 2011). The penchant for Black professionals to champion issues of 'race', or to be given the responsibility of being 'the race person' in their institution was reflected in the disparities between those involved in implementing such roles and those who are not. Further, Black women, engaged in this type of work resonated with caring, nurturing 'mammy' stereotypes, therefore being perceived differently to their Black male counterparts or White women excepted from such characterisation.

Smith and Hattery (2011) are critical of sport structures that continue the trend of poor integration of people on grounds of gender, ethnicity, nationality, sexuality or ability. The view shared by those endorsing the utopian universal 'power of sport' contradict Smith and Hattery's (2011) conclusions (Coalter 2007). Yet, what we do know about sport and society is that postracialism is not the current context, 'race', racism and other intersecting forms of oppression remain significant in sport coaching and leadership, and fractures in society are further reinforced by dominant approaches affecting decisions on who should lead and govern our sporting facilities and services (Smith and Hattery 2011).

Bias

Though many believe in the 'race'-neutral, meritocratic, 'level playing field' notions of sport they are rarely skilled enough to recognise what has been commonly described as (un)conscious bias. Unconscious bias has been used to describe the default practices used to recruit staff in sporting networks, to market to established audiences, to underpin how players are scouted, and for that matter to which sports and positions. Unconscious bias can also be used to illuminate the prevalence of microaggressions in the environment of sport that are subtle and ambiguous, yet may be manifest in even the most seemingly neutral decisions such as the choice of hospitality at events that privileges dominant cultural tastes (Long and Hylton

2002). Similarly, the images surrounding a sport or even a sport organisation can be just as effective at keeping marginalised groups away because those environments do not reflect them. They do not see anyone like themselves and therefore do not feel welcomed by those sending messages about who 'they' are and whom 'their sport' is for. Gaertner and Dovidio (2005: 619) describe these behaviours as indicative of *ingroup* and *outgroup* behaviours when they argue that,

> Many Whites who consciously, explicitly, and sincerely support egalitarian principles and believe themselves to be nonprejudiced also harbor negative feelings and beliefs about Blacks and other historically disadvantaged groups. These unconscious negative feelings and beliefs develop as a consequence of normal, almost unavoidable and frequently functional, cognitive, motivational, and social-cultural processes. [...] This mere classification of people into the ingroup and outgroups is sufficient to initiate bias.

These biases lead to conceptions of groups that draw on everyday myths, assumptions and stereotypes that abound in sport. It is exacerbated by the propensity for ingroup members to avoid association with outgroup members. Further, the more prejudiced an individual the more likely they are to avoid those in their networks with a more diverse friendship group. Such behaviours produce the closed social networks that we see manifest in recruitment and selection processes that result in the limited diversity of sport administration and leadership (Stark 2015). An ingroup mentality can also lead to inequitable expectation benchmarks for outgroup members. For example, Duru's (2011) assessment of Black coaches in the NFL found that they simply had to be more successful than their White predecessors, while after dismissal the Black coaches' teams deteriorated. Hence, hired Black coaches are consequently the most obvious best choice, with little ambiguity. It is these decisions based on merit that obscure the more ambiguous decisions that filter out competitive Black contenders. Such emphatic decisions force the hand of those with a *pragmatic racial bias* while more ambiguous decisions increase the potential for bias to succeed. Hence when Champions League winning manager Jose Mourinho argues that 'merit' rather than 'the colour of skin' is more important he confuses the problem as he conflates success with an absence of racism (Ackerman 2014).

When Kovel (1970) first emphasised two distinct forms of racism – (1) 'dominative' racism, and (2) more subtle 'aversive' racism, the complexities of racial bias and of understanding the related processes became much clearer. In sport our reactions to racial bias tend to occur in relation to more overt expressions and the chastisement of dominative racists, yet the work of Kovel (1970) and subsequently Gaertner and Dovidio (2000; 2005) forced a more critical look at those who espouse level playing field ideologies and champion notions of meritocracy. Critiquing these dispositions, practices and their outcomes enables a deeper comprehension of how racial bias can occur 'unconsciously' or 'implicitly' to influence destructive racial myths, stereotypes and assumptions.

Aversive racism is more likely to be exercised in situations that are ambiguous where there is no clear-cut approach to equity. In these moments, racial bias can be exercised without fear of recrimination for actors in sport because their unconscious or implicit biases effect racially troubling decisions. Where decision making vagaries occur and guidance is weak racial bias has exponential opportunities to be exercised. The most significant harmful effects of such behaviours are often manifest as a result of an aggregate of such acts of bias. A lack of Black and minoritised ethnic leaders, coaches, board members, officials, participants or spectators is not purely the result of one incident of racial bias though racial bias has a significant part to play in reinforcing racial disparities. For example, in the study by Norman, North et al. (2014: 21), Black coaches experienced racial discrimination in player selection processes in their formative years. The most rational and consistent variable for disparities in team selection in their formative years was 'race' and racism. This situation forced many of them to work even harder as the reality of everyday trials and tribulations made them conscious of how the world worked for them. The lack of transparency in these processes reflected the vague scenarios where racial bias can occur.

Similar to Gaertner and Dovidio (2005), the Equality Challenge Unit (2013: 1) describes unconscious bias as,

> the associations that we hold which, despite being outside our conscious awareness, can have a significant influence on our attitudes and behaviour. […] This means that we automatically respond to others (e.g. people from different racial or ethnic groups) in positive or negative ways. These associations are dfficult to override, regardless of whether we recognise them to be wrong, because they are deeply ingrained into our thinking and emotions.

The persistence of racial bias

We can begin to explain why racial biases are so persistent by understanding three processes (Gaertner and Dovidio 2005). Gaertner and Dovidio (2005) detail how the function of (a) cognitive, (b) motivational, and (c) socio-cultural processes lead to dispositions to 'race' and negative perceptions of the racialised Other that are everyday and as a result unspectacular. Their embeddedness reflects how pernicious they can be and how seriously they should be taken. They also begin to illustrate the challenge for stakeholders in sport attempting to mainstream their equalities work.

Cognitive processes lead to people in sport being categorised as belonging to 'ingroups' and 'outgroups', consequently making racial disparities a 'natural' outcome. How individuals see themselves in relation to others, and the significance of these differences, can sometimes cause a defence of the positive image of the ingroup to the detriment of the outgroup (Cunningham 2011). This construction of 'the other' has serious ramifications for social interactions, facility and service provision, recruitment and selection processes. It begins to offer insights into the value of diverse workforces where such racialised cliques are less likely to occur. It also has serious implications for the legitimation of leadership and followership, prompting questions such as *What does a leader look like? Who is viewed as an effective leader? Who is viewed as a knowledgeable leader?*

Motivational processes reflect individual or group desires to maintain status, influence and position. These motivational processes produce dominant forms of working that reproduce racialised processes regardless of sport's rhetoric of a meritocracy. Complex questions of 'race' and diversity, inclusion and exclusion, either fit these ways of working or otherwise. A defence of an individual's position in a hierarchy can occur consciously or unconsciously, yet the racial processes that lead to racial formations can occur through racial bias being allowed to flourish and remain unchecked (Omi and Winant 2002; Goldberg 2015). Resistance to equality initiatives can be partially explained by individuals reducing competition for their own jobs where the benefits of diversity have not been effectively shared. Smith and Hattery (2011) propose that a culture of White privilege is defended in sport governance and institutions that foments oppressive racial dynamics in coaching, management and other leadership spheres such as boardrooms, ultimately doing the work of maintaining status groups, structures, customs and practices that reproduce the hegemony of sporting institutions. The commercialisation of a global sport product and the neoliberal drivers of public provision have posed a major challenge in managing issues of social justice and wresting moral dilemmas out of austere environments. The hierarchy of priorities in sport organisations often leaves equality and diversity, and specific issues of 'race', relegated until key priorities of participation, performance and medals have been satisfied. Unfortunately, the nature of such priorities in sport means they are rarely satiated.

Socio-cultural processes refers to the way many in sport accept the myths and stereotypes prevalent in this contested arena. 'Race' logic that reinforces popular, if questionable racial ideologies of physical and intellectual abilities, sport and taste preferences, contributes to socio-cultural processes feeding into decisions that maintain racial formations (Omi and Winant 2002; Hylton 2015). In sport, key organisations or sport cultures retain predominantly White, male-dominated, classed and gendered institutions that haemorrhage Black players at the end of their careers or exclude them before they are able to engage more fully in leadership roles. For example, Bruno Massao and Fasting (2014) are adamant that White coaches and officials in Norway reinforce racial binaries in their coaching and officiating discussions. Norwegianness (whiteness) is reinforced as the norm while 'others' are forced to accommodate the dominant norms and cultural preferences. For example, Black athletes reflected upon how their coach would instruct them to play in a particular way against predominantly White teams because of the way officials would bias their decisions against them. Teams racialised as Black would experience what Du Bois stated what it was like to *be a problem* while the privilege of whiteness meant that the benefits accruing to White players made it unnecessary to exert any energy in considering this issue. The vicarious 'problem' accruing for those White members of teams with Black players was the subject of a study by Holland (1997), who found that spectators disproportionately insulted Black players even when the insults were non-racial. At a time when racist abuse was more explicit, in the late 1990s, overall the 'away' Black players received the bulk of abuse yet the 'home' Black players received more abuse than the away White players. Twenty years later a similar case was made by Coram and Hallinan (2017), who found that booing was used as a subtle covert device to vilify Indigenous players in Australian Football.

Dispositions to racial others

Sport can be viewed as a cultural product in the way it is perceived and reproduces the values found in wider society. Today in the UK the British Social Attitudes survey evidences that three in ten people are willing to describe themselves as 'a little' or 'very' racially prejudiced (National Centre for Social Research 2013). These statistics chart a trend over 30 years that has stayed relatively stable. This makes harsher reading when coupled with the conclusions reached by Business in the Community (2015), whose survey across Europe, the UK and the USA revealed 66–75 per cent of top executives having a racial bias, Europe performing least well and the UK relatively better than the others. More broadly, UK citizens have the lowest level of racial bias, alarmingly at 67.7 per cent, compared with citizens in Europe at over 70 per cent. Regardless of ethnicity, it was found that we all have levels of bias yet there is a difference of between 10 and 22 percentage points more White citizens categorised as racially biased than 'non-white'. In each case men are more racially biased than women and as we know full well, there are far fewer Black and minoritised ethnic men or women in senior positions in sport. Older [White] men are more likely to occupy senior positions in sport, yet older men are more likely to describe themselves as racially prejudiced (National Centre for Social Research 2013).

These statistics present serious implications for sport as those in the boardroom, and others who constitute key stakeholders in sport lead the culture of these organisations. Post-Trump and post-Brexit, more people are willing to reveal their prejudices and biases without sugaring the pill. However, such behaviours are not restricted to the current political climate of overt intolerance and xenophobia that these milestone moments have engendered. Alarmingly, the statistics above do not take into account those who do not admit to harbouring racial prejudice. For example, when Hylton and Lawrence (2016) examined the actions of ex-National Basketball Association (NBA) franchise owner Donald Sterling, they argued that he could be described as operating with an implicit, rather than unconscious racial bias because he consciously held racist views that he shared in private, in the 'backstage'. Sterling's backstage racism illustrated how the performance of liberal inclusionism in the 'frontstage' of sport can be practised at the same time as a duplicitous 'backstage' racist disposition. It is a critical eye that is able to identify and explain the difference between unconscious bias and other forms of more damaging racial biases as both can lead to significant racial disparities, the perpetuation of racial hierarchies and ideologies. Hylton and Lawrence (2016) outline that due to antiracist lobbies in sport many people will censor their racial bias for a more sanitised and socially acceptable version of themselves. This is the version that is difficult to read or implicate as dangerous in reinforcing racial discrimination and disparities. These voices are frontstage. However, Hylton and Lawrence (2016: 6) state that,

> It is in these moments, in perceived private spaces, when such actors are less guarded and backstage 'race' talk is promulgated. In the way that Goffman ([1959] 1990) argues individuals present a version of themselves […] a number of scholars have suggested that white people often discuss matters of 'race', with one another, in private spaces, differently than they would usually in the frontstage. This unwritten code of backstage 'race' talk then, wherein white people feel free to speak openly and sometimes crudely about 'race' and the racialized Other, not only challenges those who claim progress is being made regarding attitudes towards racial equality but it is significantly under-researched.

In sport, when actors are unaware of their own biases the term 'unconscious' bias is often used to describe it. However, there are times when behaviours and practices are known to frequently occur and it is at this point that 'implicit' bias should be invoked to describe behaviour that is or should be known to the per-petrators. In the case of sport, recurring issues emerge where advertisements for key leadership positions are circulated across restricted social networks. This was a key problem in the inception and acceptance of the Rooney Rule initiative in the National Football League (NFL) in America and for the pilot implementation of its equivalent in England. The Rooney Rule was established to ensure that head coach vacancies in the NFL were open to a more diverse group of candi-dates. Previously, minority [sic] coaches were being excluded and there was a paucity of Black coaches in a sport where Black players are over-represented. This initiative required at least one non-traditional minority candidate to be interviewed. Proxmire (2008) surmises that the Rooney Rule facilitates an important focus on the significance of diversity at the highest levels in the workplace. If properly implemented it ensures some resistance to unconscious bias in the workplace and that the best of everyone rather than the best of a few are considered for recruitment.

The Rooney Rule revealed impressive improvements in the subsequent years from its inception in 2002 as the number of 'minority hires' went from two to a high of fifteen in 2012 (Regan and Feagin 2017). Sanctions have been imposed to punish the Detroit Lions for contravening the Rooney Rule in 2003 although no other teams have been found wanting (Proxmire 2008). However, there still remains a relatively low number of Black NFL coaches, which demonstrates the complexity of the challenge for diversity strategies. Bias in sport must be considered alongside other multilevel concerns that affect issues of equality and social justice in sport leadership and coaching.

Sport coaching and leadership in the everyday

'Race' has been evidenced as a key influence on individual perceptions of leadership qualities. How leaders are legitimated, evaluated and treated is heavily affected by 'race' of leader or perceiver. In most cases 'race' is viewed as a limitation where ingroup and outgroup assumptions are factored into leadership decisions. Yet these assessments are layered and complex where intersections of gender, ability, even age and sexuality enter the equation. Superbowl winning coach Tony Dungy (Duru 2011: xi) remarked that one of his earliest experiences of getting into football coaching revolved around him being told quite candidly that he didn't 'look like' a coach. He recounted that,

> George Young, the general manager of the New York Giants, told me that if I wanted to have a future in coaching I needed to shave my beard. He felt I didn't look like a coach.

I myself, as an ex-coach and community sport development officer, found fewer concerns in regards to advice offered to me on personal presentation in sport leadership positions; it may seem overly intrusive but it is not uncommon for such advice to be shared. However, Dungy concluded that,

> He didn't know it but his words laid out the problem the NFL had been facing for years. There was a stereotype of what an NFL coach 'looked like', and even if I shaved, I (and other African American Assistant coaches) still wouldn't fit the perception of what owners were looking for in their coaches.

Norman, North et al. (2014: 37) found similar observations from Black coaches in the UK whose experiences led them to remain silent so that they would fit into dominant ideals of a coach. In one coach's case, he argued that,

> I think what I find is sometimes my background doesn't quite measure up to the background of somebody else, and that seems to be identifiable.

When Norman, North et al. (2014) explored the sporting experiences and coaching aspirations among Black and minority ethnic (BME) groups they revealed similar troubling issues on diversity and institutional approaches that required insight for change. British Athletics, the England and Wales Cricket Board (ECB), Badminton England and England Basketball with sixteen of their coaches, illustrated the institutional and sporting culture problems of managing diversity in sport. Each of these sports has a very diverse participation base though has struggled to replicate this superiority into notable administrative and leadership diversity. Symptomatic of an environment that reinforces the ingroup status and the privileges of whiteness approach to coach recruitment is this recollection from one of the equalities managers who noted a need for change to the current system:

I think it's getting the people that recruit coaches into the mind-set that they are looking at diverse groups … You get the same people that are recruited time and time again because you know who they are and it's not really looking at different groups who are under-represented in the sport really … I think basically the people who go out to recruit coaches they know who they are looking for to begin with and it's the same type of people that are being recruited over and over again, rather than actually going out and looking for more diverse groups of people.

(Norman, North et al. 2014: 10)

The ECB commissioned a more in-depth study after the research by Norman, North et al. (2014) to explore the barriers to South Asian cricket players' entry and progression in coaching. The study by Fletcher, Piggot et al. (2014) revealed similar issues of South Asian coaches feeling like dislocated members of 'outgroups' lacking leadership role models. Perceptions of feeling outside of a system that is 'not run for them' were manifest as dissatisfaction with systems that lacked transparency, little access to resource networks, a lack of communication, and a sense of White privilege reproducing racial differences and inequalities. The views of South Asian coaches in England in the study by Fletcher, Piggot et al. (2014: 18) found parallels in the way South Asian coaches, and experienced players, viewed their own identities as leaders and how they were racialised by key people in the game. One coach responded to the question 'can you progress as a coach?' as follows:

I can but I don't think I'll get in with Yorkshire because I still think Yorkshire pick their coaches from their skin colour.

(Coach Y2)

This coach was clearly reflecting on Yorkshire Cricket Club's controversial past condition of player entry that stipulated that their players be born in the county, thus restricting the chances of many people from diasporic Black, Asian and minoritised ethnic backgrounds. This was followed by an experienced player's view that,

I also think there's a kind of, I mean all the clubs prefer white coaches. They don't prefer south Asian coaches for the county. I mean they have a different value for white coaches.

(Player L6)

Fundamentally though, the coaches and players in Fletcher, Piggot et al. (2014) and the national governing bodies (NGBs) in Norman, North et al.'s (2014) studies recognised that there were still concerns of under-representation and poor diversity in the way their sports were led; there were negative perceptions of their sport, how leaders are viewed, and who the 'ingroups' and 'outgroups' were. In Norman, North et al.'s (2014) study, although the NGBs did monitor for ethnicity there was little analysis or rigour in the collection of data; clubs and coaches were naive about cultural differences, and they possessed an outward facing perspective to marginalised groups and issues of diversity rather than an inward, self-critical one. They also distanced themselves from significant responsibilities. The notion of responsibility or remit for equalities was directly related to resourcing rather than ethics, morals or rights. The NGBs required more extrinsic motivation. The NGBs were proactive in generic interventions to increase participation but reactive at best to issues of diversity. They lacked leadership in regards to breaking down barriers and removing the constraints that led to the loss of quality Black coaches and administrators from sport.

An inward looking, more reflexive NGB would be more likely to recognise that it should not only monitor for ethnicity but also acknowledge the lack of diversity within before then implementing the necessary interventions. It would further consider that diversity within ethnic populations can be explained with recourse to an intersectional lens that recognises that the significance of protected characteristics such as age, gender, sexuality, religion, disability in addition to 'race' should enter into considerations on participation for players, coaches and leaders. In particular, where Black women are concerned they often fall between interventions of 'race' that invariably privilege Black men, and interventions of gender which privilege White women (Jean and Feagin 1998; Hill Collins and Bilge 2016). Though the Black coaches in the study by Norman, North et al. (2014) found that their experiences of coaching were punctuated by social class, gender and ethnicity, none of the NGBs had a view on how the experiences of Black men and women coaches might differ.

Key themes from the work by Norman, North et al. (2014), Fletcher, Piggot et al. (2014), and Hylton and Rankin (2016) included coaches valuing a sporting environment where they did not feel isolated and there was a sense of diversity; there was a sense of motivation gleaned from seeing high-level coaches who looked like them; and they also felt there was a role model effect for those in local communities who were seeing Black coaches for the first time. Where they cited constraints they included (i) costs, (ii) lack of diversity, and (iii) racial discrimination. Inclusion strategies need to first identify the nature and extent of the potential problem for organisations to then be able to respond accordingly. For example, through a mixture of colourblindness and gender blindspots there remains a significant gap in comprehension as to why national governing bodies lack diversity on their coaching pathways and administration (Norman, North et al. 2014; Hylton and Rankin 2016). To further isolate how racial hierarchies are maintained, NGBs expressed the view that there was no long-term plan to recruit or retain Black coaches. The 'problem' is thus externalised and becomes the problem for Black coaches to navigate as best they can through a system that does not reflect an awareness of White privilege, racial bias, or racialised patriarchal relations.

Moving forward: racial dynamics and leadership in sport

Hogg (2001), Western (2013), and Burton and Leberman (2015) all view leadership as embedded in the social context from which it emerges. Leadership and leaders are more than the 'objective', positivistic, ideals of theorists but socially contextualised constructions redolent of their environment. Western (2013) argues that leaders and teams all work from a set of dispositions emerging from their own biographies, group experience and social location. Leaders in sport cannot detach themselves from such positions, assumptions and biases. Western (2013) uses the term *locating ourselves, to recognise the other*, and it is this critical perspective on leadership that acknowledges the racial dynamics of sport, coaching and leadership. Sport is part of the personal, cultural and structural arenas that we inhabit and operate within. They affect us as individuals and groups while in turn individuals and groups affect these broader social processes. Our relationships with and dispositions toward others are a by-product of how we move through these spaces regardless of status within them. However, sport leadership is heavily influenced by the dominant ideas within, thus our explanations for racial disparities in sport coaching and leadership need to move beyond the simple reporting of statistics.

> Activities become institutionalized when, as a result of habit, history, and tradition, they become standardized and unquestionably accepted as 'the way things are done'
>
> *(Cunningham 2010: 397)*

Tried and trusted systems of recruitment and selection can generally be relied upon to network with many of the same, or prototypes of, successful past coaches and managers; networks that are predominantly defined by whiteness that by them-selves will reproduce the profile of the constituents on the list. Puwar (2004: 8) describes such outgroup incomers as 'space invaders' as their presence emphasises a previously invisible, undeclared and unremarked somatic norm. Even if initiatives like the Rooney Rule force a re-examination of hiring practices, who leads and who governs, the fundamental reproduction of racial bias and ingrouping relies upon more mundane and seemingly rational behaviours while nefarious processes maintain their integrity. According to NFL coach Bill Walsh,

> The hiring of coaches is … a very fraternal thing. You end up calling friends, and the typical coach has not been exposed to many black coaches.
>
> *(Proxmire 2008: 5)*

It is generally agreed that the norm for leadership research has tended to reinforce perceptions that leaders are in the main male, and White (Logan 2011). Those that do not fit the prototype are absorbed into these analyses while we learn little about their qualities, experiences and diversity. The contention that Black women as leaders has been the result of little interest in the professions and in sport is the subject of debate (Sanchez-Hucles and Davis 2010). We know little about their journeys nor their specific contexts from entry to the more senior levels. The marginalisation of Black people at the highest levels of society as leaders is mimicked in sport where prototypes and stereotypes are reinforced in a recursive fashion. For Logan (2011), we still know little about how Black women manage their relative isolation, with fewer mentors and networks; what leadership qualities they may bring to these career pathways and what these strengths reveal about particular forms of leaders, character and their contribution to teams and organisations. It is understood that gender does imprint itself on perceptions of leadership, though where the synthesis of sexism and 'race' and intersecting forms of discrimination add complexity to the leadership experience is only just beginning to be understood (Borland and Bruening 2010; Sanchez-Hucles and Davis 2010). Thus, sport leadership and coaching contexts for Black women must not be viewed interchangeably with those of White women, especially as competing identities for women will manifest in different ways through uncritical views of leaders and leadership. Sanchez-Hucles and Davis (2010) add that where women face discrimination it can sometimes be more complicated for Black women to document the reasons behind their grievances as racism and gendered racism obfuscate already tortuous terrain (Carter-Francique, Lawrence et al. 2011; Bruno Massao and Fasting 2014). If White men, who in sport occupy the highest positions, are more inclined to accept White women ahead of Black women in leadership positions then not only do we see gendered racism at play but also how the beneficiaries of the privileges of whiteness can emerge at all levels of leadership pathways (Sanchez-Hucles and Davis 2010). Logan (2011: 443) argues that such dynamics describe processes that make

> White leadership appear normal, neutral, and natural, rather than the result of racialized practices … the White leader prototype is theorized as an ideological discursive formation, organising professional roles along hierarchical, racial lines.

– thus demonstrating the benefits of adopting an intersectional rather than an additive *multiple marginalised identities* analysis of leadership in sport research (Bowleg 2008). There are a number of examples where Black women and leadership has been incorporated into studies that extend our knowledge of 'race' and leadership (Sanchez-Hucles and Davis 2010; White 2010; Curtis 2014). White (2010) is an example of how inclusive research on leadership can further our knowledge of diverse leadership experiences while recognising the political contract necessary for such work to be conducted. Similarly, Curtis (2014: 62) argues that research on 'race' and leadership, especially where Black women are central, enables 'new voices' to emerge while 'sharing absent realities'. As this diversity benefits the academy while challenging its dominant epistemologies, the experiences of Black coaches and leaders become part of the leadership narrative that is valued.

Different models have been suggested to focus attention on 'race', sport coaching and leadership. A multilevel approach facilitates a specific focus on processes and practices that are simplified to locate their nature and extent (Cunningham 2010; Cunningham, Miner et al. 2012). Approaches to racial bias in sport still require a multilevel strategy. Dovidio (1993) also argues that to challenge institutional racism there needs to be a clear commitment to combatting racialised discrimination at all levels. Using the STEEP model, he outlines the following key areas for implementation: Structural support; Training; Education; Experience; Personal commitment. *Structural support* ensures that institutional resources are engaged at the highest levels to ensure that strong leadership is demonstrated. Research has shown that this is one of the key factors of excellent work in corporate equalities activities. To avoid the effects of racism in an organisation it is crucial to implement *training* and *education* to identify and combat subtle discrimination. Dovidio also points out that interracial contact can seem to be awkward and strained where aversive racism prevails. A way to challenge this state of affairs is to ensure frequent cross-cultural *experiences* and contact across organisations, and especially at the higher levels where there is poorer representation. Just as important as institutional commitment is the need for individuals to acknowledge their own *personal commitment* so they are 'part of the solution'.

Such practices cannot be left unnamed and unremarked. It is in calling out such customs and practices that organisations can become conscious of their failing processes so as to transform them. Further, the idea of *racisms without racism* (Goldberg 2008) can no longer apply in such cases where continued practices make individuals, and organisations in sport, complicit in effecting bias and its consequent impacts. In cases where practices of racialised bias continue, organisations can begin to move to more direct steps of engaging the racial disparities and racism that underpins their behaviours.

Note

1 A race equality in sport organisation.

3

FRAMING WHITENESS IN SPORT RESEARCH

> To talk about whiteness as a visible, meaningful identity with definable particularizing qualities, is to treat this category as if it were real. It is unclear at the time of this writing whether 'white studies' will embrace a critique of whiteness that challenges racial hierarchy through an explicit antiessentialist discourse, or whether it will become the vehicle through which a sophisticated, critical essentialism is articulated.
>
> *White Like Me? (Gallagher 2000: 86)*

'Race' has a direct effect on researchers, how they see and interpret the world, what research they regard as important and how they do it. This tension is rarely viewed in the way whiteness impacts how research is conducted, and further, the effects of whiteness processes and privileges on White people requires more direct consideration. Mowatt (2009) presents this as a dilemma of researcher identity and behaviour. The invisibility of whiteness in research is the reason why its practices of power for those privileged by the circumstances that reinforce racial hierarchies, dominant discourses and epistemologies are explored in this chapter. As illustrated by Gallagher (2000) above, whiteness as identity for White people is a rare consideration due to its omnipresence, invisibility and common conception that White people are not 'raced'. It is this lack of recognition of the power and influence of whiteness on research and therefore its ability to reinforce racial disparities that make it necessary for critique and implicate it as a point of resistance for antiracist, social justice oriented academics.

This chapter examines whiteness as concept, identity and process in sport and leisure research. In particular, it engenders a collective conversation with research-active scholars to reveal how individual identities impact upon how research is conducted and how racialised power is resisted, reinforced and created. While White male power dominates the academy their voices are invited here to reflect upon research on 'race' mainly because these critically reflective voices are inconsistently directly challenged or critiqued. Where authors like Gallagher (2000) find the supremacy of whiteness and White identities as conscious structurating factors, White academics are invited to speak of such issues in their approach to conducting meaningful critical work in sport and leisure (Razack 1999; Fine 2004; Blaisdell 2009; Gillborn 2011; Roithmayr 2014).

It could be argued that the supremacy of whiteness, like racism, is embedded in society and only requires ambivalence and avoidance strategies to maintain its practices. In many ways it hides in plain sight. In exploring 'race', sport and the necessary incumbent politics surrounding them, it would be a real feat not to explore the place of whiteness as a backdrop to the resilience of 'racism and notions of race' in sport and leisure research. The English lexicon is constructed in such a way as to embed racialised terms and discourses so as to render whiteness at the very worst complicit in reinforcing racial hierarchies while simultaneously innocent, beautiful and benevolent. However, evoking the very notion of 'race', blackness or 'colour' presents antitheses that render racialised entities present and conspicuous or alternatively exotic, sensual and physical (Apple 1998).

Du Bois' (1920) turn to the use of whiteness in the 1920s was to make distinct the colour coded racisms that he witnessed as an African American and social critic. Using his device of *the Veil* he utilised double consciousness to illustrate his own experiences of society and whiteness from his standpoint within the Veil. Du Bois reveals the ecosystem of race relations in the 1920s as civil society is maintained against a backdrop of a racial contract that when disrupted reveals the supremacy and power of whiteness through the subjugation of racialised people by their fellow citizens; the exploitation of Black labour by White wealth and the privileging of particular cultures and histories to the detriment of the Black other. Whiteness as supremacy and racialised identity were further revealed by Du Bois in 'The Souls of White Folk' in *Darkwater* (Du Bois 1920).

In considering whiteness, Garner (2007) offers instructive caveats in our theorisation and application of this sociological phenomenon. He warns against its generalisation, meaning and application across space where culture, nation and history offer a kaleidoscope of possibilities of interpretation of ideas over time. In sociological terms this is sound advice given the socially constructed and polysemic nature of discourses. He considers whiteness as a racialised identity, supremacy, invisible, normal, capital and contingent. Many will argue that whiteness is invisible, remains unremarked, and provides a range of unremarkable privileges to those identified as White or those able to perform a version of a White insider (Arai and Kivel 2009). In sport, whiteness discourses and practices are constructed and reproduced, requiring of us to consider more and complex ways to understand how 'race' and racism are experienced and perpetuated by all people (Roithmayr 2014).

Many years ago during a lecture with master's students I introduced findings from research that I had conducted into the nature and extent of racism in football (Long, Hylton et al. 2000). The stories that the research team heard were what led us to conclude that some of the things that White players and officials in sport did not have to contend with could be described as a privilege of whiteness. These are things that do not necessarily change the experience of taking part in sport and leisure activities, especially where this is an everyday occurrence, but when this set of unearned benefits is missing, the experiences of participants and officials in sport and leisure are qualitatively different. As we spoke about this new phenomenon one of the students said …*Whiteness? When I've been out with my Black friends to a restaurant or shop I've sometimes found that the staff treat me differently to them … now I know what to call it!* This lightbulb moment is not unusual for White adults first engaging the realities of being 'raced', having an ethnicity, or in this case benefitting from superficial physiognomical traits that have led to everyday experiences becoming qualitatively different to her friends. Though this student understood regular patterns of behaviour between her and her Black friends, the implications of these patterns and what they meant more broadly in how we navigate through structures were revealed. She glimpsed 'the Veil' for the first time to understand how others because of their minoritised status were not on a level playing field, even in leisure spaces.

White people are often regarded as having an ambivalence toward 'race', sometimes engendered by a disregard for the power and privilege of racialisation processes. This has been described as a 'dysconscious racism' that effectively leaves the privileges of whiteness and the mechanisms that maintain them undisturbed (King 1997). Not growing up with racial discourses, thoughts of 'race' affecting life chances, or without conscious racialised group identities means for many White people that the subject is avoided or replaced by forms of oppression they can empathise with (Leonardo 2009). For such people, 'race' rarely evokes a debate of whiteness due to the paucity of their critical 'race' consciousness. 'Race' then becomes synonymous with blackness and the racialised other. In this case, looking through a window becomes less challenging than looking in a mirror. Though there are many testimonies to this state of White ignorance to 'race' and racism, a simple question from Jane Elliot (2016) to White educators is telling about an intuitive White awareness of 'race', racism and privilege. Elliot asked,

> I want every White person in this room who would be happy to be treated as this society in general treats our black citizens … If you as a White person would be happy to receive the same treatment as our Black citizens do, please stand …

When no one in Elliot's auditorium stood up she countered by stating, *that says very plainly that you know what's happening, you know you don't want it for you … I want to know why you're so willing to accept it, or allow it to happen for others?* Leonardo (2009: 107) argues that it is a flawed approach to construct White people as oblivious to 'race' as it suggests notions of innocence, any recognition of the privileges of whiteness, or awareness of racial hierarchies. Working with colleagues to disrupt whiteness processes during my research has involved (a) working with students to establish some form of race consciousness, a sense of their raced self and what that implies, (b) working with institutions to establish how they perpetuate and can challenge White privilege and racial disparities, and (c) as Ignatiev (1997) said, [the point is] not to theorise whiteness processes that lead to unearned privileges, but to abolish them.

Working with White scholars

As a Black professor working regularly with White academics it has become increasingly important for us to interrogate our racialised selves in how we approach research on 'race'; to shift the binaries of *race knowers and race ignorant* so that we are all consciously implicated in racialised struggles (Leonardo 2009). Whiteness is produced by everyone. In sport we all co-produce whiteness, blackness, Asianess, Africaness, Latina/o-ness and a plethora of other identities (Fine 2004). At times these identities are performed consciously or unconsciously as ways to gain mobility and passage through hegemonic whiteness, for instance, in the arenas of sports performance, coaching and fandom (Burdsey 2004; King 2004; Ratna 2007; Ratna 2014). hooks (1999) argues that through processes of hegemonic domination and racism, Black and minoritised ethnic people may also internalise behaviours that at the same time as serving to expedite their own advancement can also reinforce racial hierarchies, stereotypes and myths of blackness and 'race'. Conversely, whiteness draws with it a sense of 'quality', 'merit' and 'advantage' more likely to benefit White people while more racialised identities *disintegrate to embody deficit or 'lack'* (Fine 2004: 246).

Sports themselves are often racialised, and it is not too challenging to think of two or three that are framed as 'White', 'Black', 'Asian' or 'African', because they are perceived to be dominated by particular social groups. Where race logic is in operation these popular myths contribute to other exclusionary mechanisms surrounding those sports. The example of skiing provided by Harrison (2013) outlines some of these mechanisms. In his critique of skiing literature and 'race' he found very few references to Black skiers over a 17-year period to 2010, even when consumer demographic profiles were the focus of debates. Skiing's social institutions, customs and behavioural practices and its rural settings interweave to result in a web of exclusion for those not traditionally associated with the sport. He considers the subtle ways in which racialised spaces function to include and then exclude, thus causing patterns of sporting segregation on racial lines. This is extraordinary in an industry suffering from a shrinking interest in the sport.

Reflexivity is important for transparency in research. The walls of pseudo-objectivity are broken down where ideas of objectivity, neutrality, colourblindnes and uncritical politics are problematised (Blair 1998). The avoidance of what Blair (1998: 13) would describe as blindspots occur as a result of researchers not being conversant with the broader historical, political and social context within which the research is conducted. When Gallagher (2000) rethought his position as a White researcher doing work as an assumed 'insider' in White communities he realised that he had entered the field with his own racialised assumptions. These assumptions led to the co-construction of a homogenised whiteness and *the White experience*. His own multifaceted whiteness and the heterogeneity of White respondents were therefore, at least initially, left uncritiqued and consequently essentialised. The project of problematising the White experience is also fraught with danger where it decentres a transformative critical race consciousness for the *possessive individualism* that has led to dominant ideas or voices being privileged (Apple 1998).

As with Gallagher (2000) the contradictions of White identities and their potential conflict of interests in research emerging from different subject positions highlights the challenges of the processes that I with my White colleagues have encountered. For example, a co-author based in Australia engaged me in a conversation on 'race', CRT and critical pedagogy with a view to publishing this dialogue. She reflected on a keynote address that I delivered where I encouraged the predominantly White audience to reflect on their whiteness by interrogating how they describe themselves (see Hylton 2009: 75). In the dialogue with me my co-author noted,

> In his seminar presentations Hylton asks participants to choose from a list of 100 adjectives (which describe personality traits), 5 items which describe the personal self, after which another 5 adjectives describing the racial self are selected. This reflective task is challenging and I circled the following adjectives to describe my personal self: 1) creative, 2) individual, 3) privileged, 4) emotional and 5) sister. When asked to describe myself racially, I chose these adjectives: A) just, B) powerful, C) puzzled, D) privileged and E) supportive. While reflecting on my choices, I couldn't help thinking about the concept of centralising 'race' and Racism in Critical Race Theory. And, if race is central to everything we do, then surely we would need to always only ever describe ourselves racially […] And at a later reflection of my role in the academy, I decided that I identify as an Applied Linguist rather than a raced/classed/gendered being, but of course race, gender, class are all aspects of me. And I know I am a non-Indigenous, white, privileged, able bodied, heterosexual, female academic living in a middle-class apartment block in a Western suburb of [State] called [Area].

Further, critical scholars who do not perceive themselves as raced are less likely to be alive to racialised power relations in the research process. They are also less likely to engage a politics of positive change in relation to 'race' where the influence of their own identities and subject positions are ignored. During the dialogue process my Australian co-author became open to viewing her racialised and complex identity as part of the research process and to recognise the privilege and power of whiteness in the study of indigeneity and the consequent Aboriginal–White Australian tensions, spinning out of their historical socio-cultural context. Being able to place her subjective self in the research process enabled her to problematise her own influence and ontology as a knowledge former. The imperialism of hidden curricula and colonisation of knowledge for indigenous people remains a threat to their cultural knowledge and a sharing of cultural experiences (Battiste 2007). Thus, she began an important decolonising project by shifting from being an *applied linguist* to being a *raced/classed/gendered being*. A paradigmatic shift for a pre-viously 'race'-neutral, 'objective' White Australian researcher conducting work with Aboriginal Australians.

With Long (Hylton and Long 2016; Hylton and Long 2017) I recognise the difficulties of working with and against racialised categories, though in acknowledging our own biographies we bear witness to our own subjectivities, perspectives and politics. Blackness and whiteness enable us to see the world in ways that enable a political race consciousness (Guinier and Torres 2003). Du Bois' ideas of whiteness and blackness are further developed in settings where both are seen as influential in their complexities that include histories, culture and politics. In doing this we state that,

> Inevitably these backgrounds shape our ontologies, social realities and the way we approach and interpret our research and data [...] We acknowledge the racialisation of our own biographies and the everyday structurating properties of pervasive racialised processes.
>
> *(Hylton and Long 2016: 202)*

With Tom Fletcher I examined the significance of whiteness as a subject of study in the sport literature over the period 2009–2015 (Fletcher and Hylton 2017; Fletcher and Hylton forthcoming 2017). In positing that White identity goes beyond skin colour and appearance, its contingent nature and the reality of the potential for its performance even by racialised others required further critique; hence leading us to the conclusion that by putting sport under the microscope as a significant cultural phenomenon we should be able to ask telling questions about the centrality of whiteness and how it affects the way we experience sport. We argued that 'race' is a paradox, that it is socially constructed and a lived reality. However, as researchers we draw on Roberts (2009: 506) to conclude that *the purpose of understanding 'race' is to recognise the power of one's own mind and status, and derive from that power the impetus necessary to reach individual and/or collective goals.* Thus, regardless of how it is accrued, where there is power there is responsibility. Our biographical differences made us further critique our thought processes for this project, policing the potential complacency that familiarity with a subject might engender. We began by reintroducing ourselves to one another by generating a pen picture of background, culture, heritage and standpoint politics.

Tom: *Tom Fletcher was born in the 1980s, in a mining town in northern England. While coming from working class upbringings, by the time his parents had started a family, they had experienced a degree of economic mobility through careers in management and self-employment respectively. Fletcher experienced what he considers to be a privileged upbringing. Relative economic stability meant that he wanted for very little – especially in sport where he was supported unconditionally. This support (alongside some talent) enabled him to represent his county at cricket from the age of 15 to the age of 21. Never acknowledging it at the time, he is now able to see how the workings of whiteness and White privilege facilitated his entry and progression in cricket. There is a general belief in most sports that to progress to higher levels of play your face must 'fit'. Fortunately for Fletcher, his did. Fletcher's White identity was shared almost exclusively by the management, coaches and team mates, thus ensuring that cricket remained a White habitus, where associated habits and tastes were normal and unproblematic. These privileges were never acknowledged but they certainly existed. Fletcher's experiences no doubt mirror those of many other White men navigating their way through the structures of sport. However, while Fletcher is now in a position to see and problematise these privileges, many others continue not to see, or are unwilling to.*

 Kevin: Hylton was born in 1960s East London to Jamaican parents who were invited to the UK with other willing members of the Commonwealth to fulfil essential jobs in under-served industries. Transport and health were the starting points for this working class family, as job security, settlement, remittances home, and navigating the overt racism of the era became their main priorities. None of this impacted the consciousness of Hylton as a youth through the school curriculum, which did not dwell on any of these issues, yet in sport, patterns emerged that only more critical reflections in later years revealed what could be described as racialised behaviours. Assumptions of natural ability in football, athletics, and cricket were flattering facilitators of insiderness and hegemonic masculinity, yet at the same time those assumptions based upon racial stereotypes were also inferring other things about intellectual capacity and propensities for success in academic as well as sporting domains. We should not be surprised that these patterns retain a certain resilience today, especially as such racialised dynamics are taxing enough to unpack for academics let alone other less critical actors in their everyday lives.

 The main themes that emerged from the study of approaches to whiteness in sport that I completed with Tom Fletcher were categorised as 'White as normal'; 'Otherness'; 'Sport Media'; 'Colourblindness'; and 'Researching whiteness'. These categories led us to conclude that whiteness critiques can be used antithetically as resistance to the prevalence of racism in sport (Garner 2007). This viewpoint is evidenced by the 'White as normal' turns to rationalise and therefore invalidate instances and experiences of racism, reflective of those with no experience of its direct harmful effects (Lusted 2009; Bradbury, Amara et al. 2011; Cunningham, Miner et al. 2012; Cleland and Cashmore 2014; Bradbury, van Sterkenburg et al. 2015). 'Otherness' in the sport literature was exemplified by ideas of racialised liminality, and Black marginality from White spaces. For example, the objectification of prominent Black sports performers in tennis and basketball, the hybridisation of South/British Asians and more latterly the realities of South/British Asian women in sport and the demystification of myths and notions of agency. Sport's propensity to facilitate social inclusion also figured in the way studies explored new migrants' access to opportunities dependent upon their degree of racialisation (Long, Hylton et al. 2014; Spracklen, Long et al. 2014).

 Linked to the theme of 'Otherness', the media's influence on developing and maintaining stereotypes and ideas of 'race' in sport has been a long-term topic for debates in the sport literature. Yet the media's role in constructing and maintaining White identities, and racialisation offline and online have become more popular areas for critique. The invisibility of whiteness and the prominence of blackness have consequently led to an ambivalence in the perpetuation of racialised ideologies in sport that leave behaviours that maintain the privileges and supremacy of whiteness undisturbed (Gillborn 2008). While White privilege and supremacy remain a threat to race relations in sport they are not shared or experienced equally by White people. Hence concerns with the contingent nature of whiteness in and through the media occupy more nuanced approaches to this phenomenon in sport (van Sterkenburg, Knoppers et al. 2010; Farrington, Kilvington et al. 2012; Farrington, Hall et al. 2015; Hylton and Lawrence 2015).

The concept of the 'invisibility of whiteness' in the media resonates with the theme of 'colourblindness' as a theoretical frame to explore whiteness (Harrison, Carson et al. 2010; Winograd 2011). Sport's meritocracy myth that reinforces notions of 'racelessness', 'post race' and 'level playing fields' has been a common focus for those critiquing how whiteness processes are maintained (Burdsey 2011). They also use these ideas to examine White privilege and racialisation in sport and sport pedagogy (Harrison 2013; Flintoff, Dowling et al. 2014). Flintoff, Dowling et al. (2014) draw this chapter back to the theme of 'researching whiteness' as the authors consider the challenges of conducting research across racialised boundaries. They centre their own White identities while drawing out the shortcomings of the paucity of a 'race' consciousness and related literature in PE and sport pedagogy. My co-author Tom Fletcher's work emerges again here to reinforce his view that,

> Reflecting critically on our biographies and positionality is the first step in recognising how whiteness operates in order that we can begin to work to disrupt it. He warns how White researchers (of sport) are, at times, culpable of reinforcing dominant racial discourses rather than challenging them; and suggests that we must consider the racialised context(s) of our own experiences and not presume that 'race' is experienced only by Black and minoritised ethnic individuals.
>
> *(Fletcher 2014: 256)*

During a critique of his own White identity Gallagher (2000) used examples of how White people have used racist talk in conversation with him as a result of their imagined kinship. Though some would say *my skin folk ain't always my kinfolk*, Gallagher found many willing to presume this was the case as they shared uncensored racist ideas with another White person. In this case skin colour and phenotype are the key criteria for insider status for those willing to engage in backstage talk. In my study with Stefan Lawrence on backstage talk (Hylton and Lawrence 2016) we examined such stories emerging through the media that demonstrated the subtle and ubiquitous qualities of this form of racism. In exploring the prevalence of backstage racism in sport it was necessary for us to outline our personal experiences of this phenomenon. It should not be surprising that my White colleague Stefan had a number of direct experiences to draw from to use as examples whereas I did not. My experiences emerged anecdotally and through our papers such as 'Reading Ronaldo: Contingent Whiteness in the Football Media' and 'For Your Ears Only! Donald Sterling and Backstage Racism in Sport' (Hylton and Lawrence 2015; Hylton and Lawrence 2016). With this backdrop we described our experiences as follows:

Hylton and Lawrence: *The two authors of this paper have very different biographies and therefore divergent experiences of frontstage and backstage 'race' talk. Hylton has a black colonial heritage born of parents arriving in 1950s London not to find 'streets paved with gold'. In fact they were 'welcomed' with signs in guest-house and hotel windows, and other public spaces, warning 'Blacks need not apply'. A child of the 1960s and 1970s, 'race' has always been an imposition, and central, to his identity, though the nature of the racism experienced by his parents has metamorphosed into more sophisticated versions today. Hence, examinations of racialised dynamics and 'race' are necessarily an ontological starting point for research especially in what is often described as the meritocracy of sport.*

Lawrence was also born in England, during the 1980s, though has a mixed white-European heritage (see also Lawrence 2014). At variance with Hylton's recollections, Lawrence cannot recall feeling the matter of 'race' affected his childhood: he cannot remember being told that his achievements as a child were a result of anything but hard work; and never was he made to feel that he was 'minority ethnic', despite his father's family having migrated from Italy/Sicily in the early 1950s. Therefore, although he was aware of subtle ethnic differences between himself and his peers, he was never marked as having a racial identity or as being significantly (read: racially) different from the majority of his peers, teachers, or sport coaches.

Being read corporeally, and thus racialised, as White had granted Lawrence access to a number of privileges that were and are often reserved for those admitted to the 'private club of whiteness' (Jensen 2005). A positive association (determined largely somatically and thus, in some cases, unknowingly) that grants members, not only privilege but also, access to a number of restricted, private spaces, often reserved for White people or particularly 'deserving' Others. One such arena is in the backstage, a private space wherein a seemingly forgotten form of whiteness and racism festers. [...] And so, despite his political and ideological opposition Lawrence has been routinely 'witness to whiteness' in the backstage (Fine 2004; Hylton and Lawrence 2016: 5).

Recognising backstage talk and being willing to challenge it directly or critically in writing means taking steps that acknowledge (a) the prevalence of racism(s), (b) that whiteness is implicated within racist structures, and (c) that White privilege and experiences are contingent (Long, Hylton et al. 2014; Hylton and Lawrence 2015). Contingency and White privilege and experiences are situated, contextual and reflective of multiple identifiers. The embodied intersecting identities for Lawrence and my other White colleagues included their sex, gender, age, class, northern and southerness, abilities, politics, and nationalities. It is a necessary requirement for them to problematise simplistic notions of White insiderness while recognising the politics and pragmatics of lived identities and realities outlined by Gallagher (2000).

Whiteness has been explored further in order to move beyond more obvious analyses that tempt one to lean more heavily on binaries that lead to reductionist conceptions of Black and White. In earlier work with Long and Spracklen (Long, Hylton et al. 2014) and Lawrence (Hylton and Lawrence 2015) I examined the way whiteness was experienced differently across the socially constructed and het-erogeneous social group described as White people. Between us we explored how whiteness processes were contingent on a number of situated and social factors that emphasised racialised hierarchies within this group that in reality benefit from

White privilege in an uneven fashion. With Long and Spracklen (Long, Hylton et al. 2014) our analysis of White new Polish migrants revealed the way whiteness was unconsciously recognised as a factor that could assist the settlement process (see also Spracklen, Long et al. 2014). Whiteness was viewed as a form of capital that in some cases was perceived not to have as much impact on chances of integration when Polish-English was made public and revealed 'difference' in established community spaces. Similarly through the use of media images the perception of Portuguese and Real Madrid soccer star Cristiano Ronaldo by White English males in the study with Lawrence (Hylton and Lawrence 2015) is clearly viewed as a 'different' and peripheral kind of White man due in the main to the way he performs his high-profile and elaborate 'metrosexual' masculinity. Ronaldo's ethnicity and nationality were called into question by these English men as masculinities and xenophobic tendencies further exacerbated his White 'otherness'.

In the paper on leisure and the integration of new migrants (Long, Hylton et al. 2014) we drew on the case of White Polish migrants to explain how whiteness is not monolithic. The work of Satzewich (2000) emphasises how whiteness is far from fixed and rigid but more fluid due to space, time, individual and group particularities, and various interpretations. The peripheral nature of Whiteness in England was examined as sport and leisure were used as vehicles for the integration of Black Africans and White Polish migrants. In the study we found that the Black Africans were aware that being Black was enough to be othered yet the subtle difference with their Polish counterparts compared to the White host community was that they found that being White was not quite enough to prevent this process of othering from happening. To a degree the symbolic capital of whiteness facilitated access and inclusion into established community spaces. Access to the invisible knapsack of White privilege (McIntosh 1988) being accrued was more clearly apparent in the way the Polish migrants moved through public spaces more easily and comfortably than the Black African migrants; this was emphasised by Polish migrant Rafal, whose penchant for integration into English culture was piqued. He stated,

> I say to my wife that we are in England and we need to try to be like English … we can't be shouting out in the shop or the bus because people will not understand, they will be confused if we shout out in Polish … we keep the Polish tradition at home. We try to look like an English … not a Polish people … *just normal like the people who are living here … the local.*
>
> *(Long, Hylton et al. 2014: 1790)*

Even though the Black African migrants felt more clearly racialised, othered, and marked out as different, the Polish migrants were still racialised and *differently Othered or discriminated against* as social and cultural capital intersected with whiteness and the racialisation of sport and leisure spaces (Long, Hylton et al. 2014: 1781). Rafal and his wife were conscious of the need to fit in by using the symbolic capital of whiteness, developing their and their children's English language and, at least in public, relegating their Polish origins. Their recognition of feeling minoritised and on the periphery of the local community led to strategies that would help them become more English than Polish, especially for their children beginning school in a new country.

For both the Polish and African migrants the work of bridging networks in new communities made some of them spend more sport and leisure time with other migrants to help them relax in environments where they did not need to use as much effort to be themselves. These strategies suggest that migration for Black and White migrants have similarities and differences that are nuanced and not purely reducible to blackness and whiteness, as language, nation, gender, class affect the explanations mooted for the quality of settlement and integration of Black and White migrants. It is clear that blackness and contingent whiteness are specific and significant factors in processes of migration and integration in sport and leisure arenas. We found that,

> Polish migrants have to work harder at the performativity of whiteness than do white British people – our research participants may be white, but are not yet 'white' in British society.
>
> *(Long, Hylton et al. 2014: 1793)*

My White colleagues drew on similar experiences of whiteness regardless of the focus of our work on 'race'. The most detailed and focused illustration of this came in a reflective study with Jonathan Long. In one paper we posited that,

> We write from a UK perspective as one Black and one White researcher and know from our own biographies the complexity and shortcomings of such categories.
>
> *(Hylton and Long 2016: 1)*

These complexities were explored in '"Knowing Me, Knowing You": Biographies and Subjectivities in the Study of "Race"' (Hylton and Long 2017). In this paper we considered how in a larger study with two other academics we explored the influence of 'race' on how we conducted research. We went through a process of writing a detailed biopic that the others critiqued. "Knowing me, Knowing you" enabled us to reflect upon our bios from the initial larger study. While reflecting on how 'race' structures a researcher's approach to studying 'race' our racial selves were brought into sharp relief. I reflected upon incidents that caused my own double consciousness to be awakened in primary school, while for Jonathan it became more about the asymmetry in our stories.

Jonathan: *Born in Calcutta where my father worked for 10 years after 'Independence'. Parents were members of the social and sports clubs, but I had little awareness of the social significance of these until much later. We left when I was four so have few clear memories. However, it left some trace because for as long as I can remember any political consciousness, and predating any theoretical analysis, I've been uncomfortable with the colonial legacy ...*

We returned to a very White Norwich. I doubt I saw a Black person in the city the whole time I lived there [...]

While aware of difference, my appreciation of Whiteness was slow to develop. At first this is hardly surprising. Even when we moved to Huddersfield [aged 13 in 1966] where there were Black people from African-Caribbean communities, they played little part in my life. There was both spatial segregation, we lived on the edge of town, and educational segregation, I went to a boys' (state) grammar school. I have no clear recollection of there being African-Caribbeans in the school, and can only remember there being three Asians. Moreover, although we played ordinary rugby rather than 'rugger' I have no memory of playing against school teams with Black players either. My awareness of whiteness only arose while travelling abroad, which is something easily left behind in the quotidian of daily life in the UK.

Jonathan went on to write that in comparison with my account, his reflection points to the asymmetry in racialisation between Black awareness of blackness and White awareness of whiteness; few people in African Caribbean or Asian communities can be so forgetful. Co-researchers in the original study observed that Jonathan's appreciation of difference involved an intermingling of class and nation rather than of matters purely of 'race'. In relation to the notion of a 'racial awakening' Jonathan felt it was more evolutionary over a period of time, though regardless of the process he recognised his own privilege. He went on to state,

As a member of staff in a university my privileged position allows me to promote anti-racist messages [...] During the course of our research into racism in sport I have felt that it is easier for me to expose elements of racism than it is for Black researchers in the same field. My critiques cannot so readily be dismissed as special pleading (a Black researcher might be accused of having a chip on their shoulder), but I've still been accused of finding what I want to find, seeing racism where it doesn't really exist. Well, I can take that.

Conclusion

The White glaucoma that has ruined scholarly vision that Fine (2004: 246) writes of is one explored and explained here. It is visible to some but unfortunately not to all. The power of whiteness and its seductive invisibility requires a critical eye and 'race' conscious lens that some of my White colleagues have challenged themselves to operationalise. This chapter explores whiteness and its dynamics in research. It is revealed as a complex concept, not uniformly experienced by White people just as it is contingent, invisible, often unremarked, open to different meanings over time and space, the norm, a racialised identity, privilege and supremacy (Garner 2007; Hylton and Lawrence 2015; Fletcher and Hylton 2017). Issues of 'race' in sport are often squarely focused on blackness, yet the necessity to implicate whiteness in conversations on 'race' and racism, racial processes and racial projects is unavoidable if meaningful change is to be achieved. How whiteness impacts the way White scholars approach their work is part of this project, and it is revealed in how it influences their stocks of knowledge and identities. They have acknowledged that the approach they take to their research and what that means to them in terms of disrupting racial power relations is an ongoing reflexive exercise that, as

Rollock (2013) demonstrates, even the most conscious of researchers must remain vigilant about to maintain their own antiracist and transformative agendas.

Whiteness processes made visible in sport research recognises that as social researchers the myth of 'race' neutrality, colourblindness and objectivity skew the quality of the knowledge that we generate and inherit. Research and research environments become more diverse and representative of those traditionally on the margins. However, for those at the centre or periphery of whiteness the privilege of whiteness cannot be underestimated, ignored or used irresponsibly. As whiteness discourses and practices can be constructed and produced to reinforce racial disparities they can also be challenged from the inside, frontstage or backstage, by those conscious of its omnipresence and effects.

4

A PRISON OF MEASURED TIME?

'Race', sport and leisure in prison

> Research specifically concerning the role of sport in prisons and with offending populations remains sparse, despite the obvious lessons that may be drawn from the more established practices in community settings and the additional opportunities and uses for sport in the context of incarceration and rehabilitation.
>
> (Meek 2014: 1)

Sport for Marxist Jean-Marie Brohm (1989) emphasises the control of the state in how we access and play sport. For Brohm (1989) self-empowerment through sport is an illusion perpetrated by an insidious state monopoly. When Brohm (1989) described sport as *a prison of measured time* he was taking as his cue the instrumental and mythopoetic elements of sport-related activity in society. For him sport is repressive but a critical way in which people relate to their bodies. In a prison, sport can be used as a way to represent self, a technical means to an end, a symbolic depiction of productivity, a site of diversion and a transmitter of ideological values. Martos-Garcia, Devis-Devis et al.'s (2009) work on prisons and sport draws similar conclusions on the meaning of prison sport[1] as multidimensional. Social control, escapism and catharsis emerge as relatively predictable themes given the literature on the benefits of sport. Yet the authors identify other characteristics of sport that give meaning to prisoners, which include the performance of masculinity. Others have drawn similar conclusions and debated the potential of sport and physical activity to break down barriers while offering health, 'adjustment' and other benefits (Meek and Lewis 2012; Meek and Lewis 2014; Parker, Meek et al. 2014). Some of these benefits have revolved around social capital developed through engagement and participation in sport and physical activity. This chapter explores the significance of 'race' in the way prisoners engage in sport and recreation.

To explore some of these issues, the chapter draws on a prison study in the north of England, with a view to understanding what sport means for prisoners and what import 'race' may have on this process. The study considers findings from fieldwork with Black and minoritised ethnic (BME) and White prisoners, physical education instructors, and senior governing officers in a low risk prison; prisons are divided into categories of risk from A (high) to D (low/open). The prison that is the focus of this research is category C. Martos-Garcia, Devis-Devis et al. (2009) support the view that more research is necessary to understand core practices in prison life so as to have a stronger and more realistic grasp of the challenging daily processes that prisoners have to manage. The prisoners' use of sport becomes one of the factors that contributes to establishing a routine. It also becomes a factor that is imbued with meaning and potential physical, psychological and social benefits, not so well researched in the prison and sport literature. The implications for practice are manifold in regard to the prison service having a much clearer grounding of the personal and environmental drivers for participation in sport, its various settings and social outcomes. To understand these processes and practices is to begin to reduce the potential for ineffective practice, and facilitate wellbeing through enabling those characteristics of sport and physical activity that prisoners recognise as productive, positive and worthwhile.

The use of sport and physical education as social drivers, key to socialisation, social control, and crime prevention, has a long and contested history (United Nations 1955). For example, Andrews and Andrews (2003) outline the competing ways that sport has been viewed over time by different stakeholders. Some see sport in prisons as out of place because it should be a place for punishment, while others advocate a need for the rehabilitative and humanitarian promise of sport and physical education. Links between sport and physical education and the cultural development of nation states have varied histories but there is no denying their utility over time as vehicles to underpin the norms, values and mores of nations. In regard to the possible benefits of sport, Coalter (2007) outlines five main themes underpinning interventions that include improved fitness and health, mental and psychological wellbeing, personality development and self-esteem, social psychological improvements, and sociological effects on relationships with others. Carney and Hardwick's work for the PE Services Operational Services and Interventions Group with the National Offender Management Service (NOMS) for the Butler Trust (2014) affirms such practical benefits of sport provision in prisons as they describe safe environments that improve discipline, order and control, violence reduction and diversion, with secondary benefits of improved education and training outcomes (Meek and Champion 2012).

However, resource constraints affect the sustainability of exemplars of good practice case histories, PE staff expertise is limited in regards to gathering substantive evidence, and the limited ability to track prisoners after release has been a major constraint in establishing the impact of interventions on their readjustment. Further, it could also be argued that the nature of sport with its explicit rules, regulations and restrictions may make them unattractive to those seeking more unconventional or antisocial forms of stimulation. The sociology of sport has been part of the 'echo of critique' advocated in the preface to Brohm's (1989) work that calls for a necessary criticism of sport and its place in state institutions. Sport, for Brohm

(1989) represents a major blindspot in the social consciousness, because sport for him remains a major tool of state repression, imprisonment if you will, thus making a challenge for critics to render sport's ideological and socio-political meaning visible. Sport has been described as a site of liberation and constraint, yet in this chapter, the prison is the ultimate tool of state control that frames the sport provided in a deliberate way and seemingly 'chosen' within these constraints by prisoners. In this sense the dualism of freedom and constraint is writ large. The very notion of control is central to how prisons work to frame the experience of prisoners; although how sport opportunities are experienced within this is subject to conjecture (Norman 2015).

Ethnicity has been argued to be a major factor affecting how people access, engage and experience sport and leisure. Issues of inclusion and exclusion within and across identified ethnic groups is a significant aspect of this work. However, it has not been the consistent focus of attempts to critique the place of sport in prisons beyond a few notable exceptions (Meek and Champion 2012; Meek 2014). Further, in this dearth of published works scant attention has been paid to specific issues concerning the dynamics of 'race' and sport that might ask the questions *What are the conditions of participation in sport for racialised prisoners?* and *What does it mean for over-represented ethnic populations and those charged with managing their rehabilitation and residence?* Similarly, the conflicted prison as an empowering and constraining influence on sport, physical activity and PE will be explained.

Prison in context

The world prison population stands at over 10.35 million (Walmsley 2016). Since 2000 the world population has increased by approximately 20 per cent. In Europe there has been a significant increase, with Spain recording one of the largest (Martos-Garcia, Devis-Devis et al. 2009). The prison population in England and Wales has risen steadily since the end of the Second World War and currently stands at around 84,000 (Berman and Dar 2013). Of that prison population the mixed, Asian/Asian British, and Black/Black British are heavily over-represented, making up approximately 25 per cent of the total population (Berman and Dar 2013: 11). Muslim prisoners are also represented at over three times their 4 per cent of the general population. Where Phillips and Webster (2014) recognise the significance of 'race' in the criminalisation of Black communities, one of the topics rarely included in these debates is the significance of sport in the lives of this over-represented population of the prison system. The Ministry of Justice (2010) statistics on race and the criminal justice system states that the prison population in England and Wales is heavily over-represented by BME prisoners. This state of affairs is replicated in the United States where Black people are five times more likely to be incarcerated than White people and similarly, Hispanic people are twice as likely to be incarcerated as White people (Sakala 2014). In France, the government does not monitor for ethnicity but rather citizenship. The French Ministry of Justice is able to state that 82 per cent of its prison population is French and the other 18 per cent have their country of origin publicly stipulated (Kazemian and Andersson 2012). Thus, the demography of a French prison population is not definitive in regards to ethnicity. However, some estimates have 60–70 per cent of the c.68,000 prison population composed of Muslim prisoners whereas Muslims make up only 12 per cent of the whole population (Moore 2008; Alexander 2015).

In the prison where this study takes place, 26 per cent of the prisoners are from a BME background compared to 12 per cent in the general population (ONS 2011). The criminal justice system (CJS) is charged with correction and rehabilitation for prisoners yet we know little about how sport and leisure experiences contribute to this. Gabbidon and Taylor Greene (2005) argue that a type of self-fulfilling racial ideology can be evidenced in the way race and crime are associated. This race logic is underpinned by racism's dynamism and ability to shift and change over time. They go on to outline waves of racial ideologies in perceptions of 'race' and crime. A first wave defended the notion that criminal Blacks have the innate propensity to break the law and therefore deserve incarceration. Following on from this idea a second wave supports the view that such disproportionately high numbers of Black and minoritised ethnic prisoners 'prove' that the assumptions of the first wave were correct.

Crime, 'race' and blackness

The prison system in England and Wales has had a chequered history where 'race' and racism are concerned. In the wake of the Stephen Lawrence Inquiry (Macpherson 1999) that found incontrovertible evidence of institutionalised racism in the London Metropolitan Police, the Commission for Racial Equality's investigation into three prisons in England and Wales came to similarly damning conclusions (CRE 2003). The inquiry into unlawful discrimination lasted 3 years (2000–2003) and reported on the state of race relations in HMP Brixton, HMP Parc and YOI Feltham. There were fourteen key areas of failure across the prisons that included a discernible culture that engendered racial abuse, harassment and victimisation while racial equality procedures were ignored. The prison staff and prisoners were subject to forms of racism that included a physical environment depicting racial graffiti while racially taunted staff were left unprotected by rules and regulations, often left to deal with incidents by themselves. Sometimes the victims of racism were transferred to even more strict prisons, thus leaving them with a double burden. Further, both staff and prisoner complaints left them subject to victimisation and further harassment. A culture of whiteness and White privilege was allowed to develop while racialised inequalities and marginalisation were left unfettered. This racist discourse is what Davis (2001) describes as criminalised Black male bodies being treated as dispensable.

Significantly from a sport and wellbeing perspective, Black prisoners were regularly overdisciplined and discriminated against in relation to their access to goods, facilities and services. Many religious, non-Christian groups, in particular Muslims, were regularly under-served with unsatisfactory access to their religious requirements. Racial ideologies of prison staff led to assumptions and stereotypes that systematically punished Black prisoners and regularly (discretionally) took leisure time away from Black prisoners by leaving them in their cells. The lack of ethnic monitoring across the prisons meant that these patterns could be easily ignored or glossed over due to the paucity of substantive evidence. The later Human Rights Approach to Prison Management advocated by the International Centre for Prison Studies (ICPS) states the need for diversity to be recognised and for prison authorities to eschew the dated notion of prisoners being a homogeneous group and of the same dominant ethnic or religious category (Coyle 2009). The ICPS go on to argue,

> Many of the prejudices which exist in society against minority groups are reflected in the world of the prison. This is no surprise since prisons to a great extent mirror the values of the society in which they exist. Prison authorities have a duty to ensure that there is no discrimination against any minority group of prisoners or staff or any religious group. This includes institutional discrimination which is within the structure of the organisation as well as discrimination which is practised by individuals.
>
> *(Coyle 2009: 117)*

It is worth noting that the common use of the term Black for Earle and Phillips and other social commentators such as Modood (1994) has broken the hegemony of the inclusive content of its original usage and therefore requires a re-evaluation and recognition of the breadth of specific identities. Even though Modood (1994) recognises the need to group together those who suffer racial discrimination and marginality as a result of the colour, culture and heritage the argument for a collective mobilisation of these populations using this term still causes harm to (British) Asian populations. Particularly on the basis of false essentialism, the overbearing nature of 'everyday blackness', and a loss of cultural identities there remains a need to recognise the shifts in the politics of 'race' and racial identity. Terms reflective of heterogeneity and political collectivity require a sensitivity not always manifest in everyday discourse. Yet embedded in this political project lies the danger of a conflation of struggles and the homogenisation of identities and experiences. In light of the prevalence of Islamophobia and the conspicuously concerted efforts of law enforcement to target stereotypes of Muslim/Asian/Arab-ness it is imperative to recognise specific and collectivist uses of terms.

Earle and Phillips (2013) raise the awful spectre of racial inequalities in levels of incarceration. They make the harrowing observation that the Anglo-Welsh prison system imprisons disproportionately higher levels of Black people than even the United States. The Ministry of Justice (2015) supports this in their analysis that focused on the associations between ethnic background and being sentenced to prison in the Crown Court in England and Wales, where they concluded,

> For offenders convicted of recordable, indictable offences in the Crown Court in 2015, there was an association between ethnicity and being sentenced to prison. Under similar criminal circumstances the odds of imprisonment for

offenders from self-reported Black, Asian, and Chinese or other backgrounds were higher than for offenders from self-reported White backgrounds.

(Ministry of Justice 2015: 1)

Across the whole prison population of 86,000 prisoners 95 per cent are men (82,000) and 5 per cent are women (4,000) (Ministry of Justice 2016: 109). Though there has been an increase of White and BAME (Black, Asian and minority ethnic) male prisoners there has been a decrease of female prisoners of 3 per cent White and 42 per cent BAME. In sum, there are some distinct differences concerning ethnic populations between men and women since 2005 (Ministry of Justice 2016). Up to 2015 there was an increase of 9 per cent for White women yet a decline of 1 percentage point to 73 per cent for White men even though for males there has been an overall increase between 2005 and 2015. Due to the significance of the male proportions across the prison population the overall proportion of White prisoners fell by 1 percentage point (to 74 per cent – 63,000). The Ministry of Justice for England and Wales' *Equality Report* for 2015/16 (Ministry of Justice 2016) emphasises the disproportionate representation of Black and minoritised ethnic prisoners. In 2011 the Ministry of Justice illustrated the proportionate differences in ethnic representation across the prison population (Ministry of Justice/National Offender Management Service 2011).

Prison: a total institution

Fortune and Whyte (2011: 25) observe a process of marginalisation that occurs when people transition into prisons. This involves a break with personal and community social networks, segregated institutional interactions, and a loss of role and identity. This marginalisation is described by Fortune and Whyte as *the most dangerous form of oppression*. Institutions like prisons are intriguing points for sociological analysis because they elevate the idea of institutionalisation to a point that is all embracing. Goffman (1961) would argue that they should be described as *total institutions*, as depicted by their falling into one of five categories of a total institution. Prisons fall into category three:

> A third type of total institution is organised to protect the community against what are felt to be intentional dangers to it, with the welfare of the persons thus sequestered not the immediate issue: jails, penitentiaries, P.O.W. camps, and concentration camps.
>
> *(Goffman 1961: 17)*

A significant aspect of total institutions is that they depart from common social arrangements in the way we eat, sleep, work and play under different authorities, rules and regulations. Prisoners are regulated under the same rules, same authority, same people, same routines, and in the same place: aspects of which we see in all institutions but rarely all together. Within the total institution of prisons, social relations are subject to sustained fissures, sometimes tense and regularly on the social–antisocial continuum. In particular, prisoner–staff relations tend to be functional, with issues of trust, conflict and hostility commonly affecting these social dynamics. Within certain parameters, prisoner–prisoner relations are reflective of other institutional dynamics, though are exacerbated by convenience, function, survival, surveillance and exclusion. Just as with work, where full reward is minimised for a day's labour then so is access to sport and PE. Goffman (1961) argues that just as an adjustment needs to be made to prisoner motivation to the rewards, type and availability of work then in principle so too will there need to be reassessments of the value and function of sport for prisoners and prison officials. Further, the relationship between work and sport, where sport is often elided as a complementary relief and change of pace to work, becomes an interesting tension to explore (Bramham 2002; Rojek 2005).

The significance of sport in a prison is heightened by its place in the system of privileges fundamental to the running of a prison. Goffman's (1961) description of the privilege system incorporates a collective set of elements to be balanced, that includes the prison's (i) 'house rules', (ii) rewards and privileges for adhering to element (i), which include sport and other free time activity, and (iii) punishments for contravening element (i). In the outside community our sport is a privilege accessed at leisure, when most beneficial to the recipient and generally at times convenient to the participant. Where basic conditions are met, such as participation fees, beyond certain exception, sport cannot legally be withheld. In a prison, access to sport is conditional on meeting certain demands of the institution. Good behaviour is rewarded and behaviour that falls outside of these parameters is punished. Staff–prisoner and prisoner–prisoner relations must remain convivial to ensure that the prison ecosystem is maintained. Access to such privileges requires of prisoners a particular mode of behaviour before, during and after sport participation to ensure that sport and other privileges are maintained. A consideration of the way sport is experienced in prison must take into account this dynamic and how it may impact the quality of activities engaged.

Norman (2015) suggests that prisoners refashion the implicit social control agenda of sport, using it to resist and disrupt the hegemony of the institution. In prisons, where actors are under constant surveillance and regulation, sport and PE can offer a level of freedom of expression even within its 'prison of measured time', for purely autonomous behaviours, movement, speech, control and reinterpretation of rules (of the game). In ways not regularly supported in the everyday routine of prisons the catharsis of sport is both physical and psychological. In such an environment, it could be argued that the traditional benefits of sport for those in prison take on a different meaning to their civil society identities. For example, Martos-Garcia, Devis-Devis et al. (2009: 82) argue that a lesser known benefit of sport in prison is its function of *filling in, occupying or passing time*.

As Goffman (1961: 47) posits, 'a margin of self-selected expressive behaviour [...] is one symbol of self-determination'. Yet, where sport is considered with binaries such as work-sport (work–leisure) we also see for prisoners that there is a clear association with punishment (limited/no sport) and with privilege (access to sport). In total institutions like prisons there is a constant negotiation of these binaries that elevate the place of sport and therefore its significance, in the life of all prisoners. Levels of agency are manifest in sport that confound theoretical ideas of prisoner experiences of such institutions. For example, access to sport may be perceived as an indicator of rehabilitation where it reflects regularly accrued privileges redolent of a model prisoner. In some cases the time of release is predicated upon the institutional privilege system (Burns 1992). Goffman (1961) argues that this tension in prisons is necessarily maintained as a form of leverage in the management of prisoners. In parallel to this, rule-bending and resistance to staff demands, in a sporting context, illuminate the potential for sport as a vehicle for more subversive functions. Norman (2015) describes these functions as part of the everyday *underlife* of prisons that might use sporting spaces as opportunities for commerce, violence, drug use or shows of strength and masculinity. These processes are compounded by the manifestation of what Sabo (2001) describes as a patriarchal institution. According to Sabo, Kupers et al. (2001) the absence of women, where male–male contact is the norm, the prevalence of hierarchies, and the threat of violence are the four earmarks of patriarchal institutions.

Sport and identities

Sport is an arena in which masculinities are manifest and tested (Messner and Sabo 1990). Male prisons are one of the atypical male spaces where symbolic masculinities are enacted, or even exaggerated, especially as a process of emasculation occurs on entry (Sabo 2001; Ricciardelli 2015). Bandyopadhyay's (2006) research in India explains that on incarceration a prisoner's identity shifts on losing their independence, worker and family status, and even community or individual prestige. Sporting contexts reify this as Whitson (1990) describes them as testing grounds for redefining self and demonstrating manliness or *being male*. For many in prison, weight training or physical activities to enhance body strength or demonstrate power have been viewed as vehicles to construct particular forms of masculinities and enhance self-esteem and positive peer recognition (Phillips 2012). Coupled with peer and institutional pressures, such identities have been seen to shift prisoner perceptions of different forms of masculinity. Some of these pressures emerge through a more specific use of the notion of patriarchy, in prisons, to one that reflects power demonstrated by men through fraternities (fratriarchy) and hierarchies (Jewkes 2005; Phillips 2012; Ricciardelli 2015). Significantly, Bandyopadhyay (2006: 188) emphasises that alternative forms of masculinity can be performed at strategic times of a prisoner's journey through the system as they attempt *to reclaim agency and assert a sense of self*. However, forms of symbolic masculinity and the threat of individual and group strength and/or resistance in the prison system has led to some justice systems changing the type of access to free weights or contact sports (Norman 2015). Norman (2015: 10) goes on to argue that in addition to the use of the gym and physical activity spaces to construct individual and gang identities and hostile environments,

> Prisoners lift weights for a variety of reasons, including improving physical health, taking control over one's body, *becoming more intimidating to guards and other prisoners, deterring violence against oneself*, self-improvement and goal setting, managing boredom, socializing with friends, managing stress, and *making oneself useful as 'muscle' in a gang.*
>
> *(My italics)*

Richmond and Johnson (2009) argue that the underlife of prisons is predicated upon survival and that 'race' is central to what they call racially organised prison politics. These decisions include how leisure time is spent, where, and with whom based upon unwritten prison mores, norms and peer pressure. They found that leisure decisions were the result of levels of indoctrination, maintenance and structural support that reinforced an institutionalised, racially underpinned hegemony. This hegemony was endorsed by the bureaucracy that ignored the conspicuous racial dynamics by maintaining a neutral position. The common lack of concern about how people spend their leisure time and whether some feel more comfortable in the free time with individuals from particular backgrounds can lead to a perpetuation of distance across racial lines (Du Bois 1994). The reproduction of racialised spaces leads to implicit boundary markers between social groups and increased marginalisation. As seen in the past, racial processes and formations from outside prison institutions and in our freely chosen sport and leisure time may shift and can be reimagined in the new prison arena (Hylton and Morpeth 2012; Long, Hylton et al. 2014; Spracklen, Long et al. 2014). Alternatively, Phillips (2012) outlines instances where ethnic differences can be negotiated where inclusivity is fostered due to proximity, and positive social relations emerge through an everyday cultural education. In the case of Phillips' (2012) in-depth study of Rochester Young Offenders' Institute and Maidstone Category C prison, though there was racism in the prisons, she found that racial and religious disparagement was recognised as a line not to be crossed by prisoners.

Methodology

The principal research focus for the fieldwork was to explore the significance of 'race' in how prisoners engage with and perceive the benefits of sport and physical activity. It involved (1) three mixed ethnicity prisoner focus groups with a total of twenty-two in attendance. From a total population of 815 there were approximately 185 BME prisoners in this prison. Prisoners were invited to voluntarily participate; of these over a third were BME (see Table 4.1); (2) one focus group with PEIs (physical education instructors); (3) one interview with the Custodial Manager, who was the PEI's line manager; and (4) one interview with the Head of Reducing Reoffending, who was the line manager for the Custodial Manager.

TABLE 4.1 Ethnic breakdown: prison focus groups

Focus group	White	Black	Mixed	S. Asian
1	5	1		2 (Pakistani and British Muslim)
2	4		1	1 (Pakistani Muslim)
3	5			3 (British Pakistani) (2 Muslim/ 1 no religion)
Total = 22	14 White	1 Black	1 Mixed	6 S. Asian

As with many studies in prison settings the need for security meant that prisoners were unable to be left to speak unconstrained in complete privacy. It also required a risk assessment to ensure that prisoners were able to freely and voluntarily contribute to the focus groups. As a result, prisoners were accompanied by a PEI who waited outside the room to enable a more relaxed and open exchange with the researcher. As with any study of prisons there were a number of ethical considerations:

1. Prisoners fall into the category of 'vulnerable' or 'high risk' and hence questions avoided reinforcing the ongoing stigma of incarceration or feelings of guilt.
2. Similarly, a focus on 'race' had the potential to lay bare sensitive issues in an environment that has been evidenced to reify these differences in a destructive fashion. In addition, 'race' has explicitly been analysed as a fault line among prisoners in previous studies and therefore questions were carefully chosen to prepare the prisoner for such exchanges.
3. Though there is always a risk in a prison setting this was in a lower risk Category C institution.
4. There are no guarantees that prisoners would have finished formal education or be functioning at an average literacy level if they have been in the system for a while. Hence consent forms were written to ensure that all interviewees had an equal chance to understand the purpose of the study and their contribution to it; such an approach lends itself to transparency. In addition, before the start of each focus group the interviewer read out the Participant Information and Consent form details before collecting signed consent.
5. Meek (2014) pragmatically recognises prisoner definitions of sport as they may not have a nuanced understanding of the differences between physical activity, exercise and sport as defined by the Department of Health.
6. Anonymity: Included in the consent form was a disclosure for maintaining anonymity, confidentiality and security.

The gym facilities

There are two gyms in this prison. The main gym is redolent of an aging council community sport centre. Walking into the gym it takes some time for the eyes to adjust to the dated lights that struggle to offer the brightness associated with a modern facility. This is more of a traditional 1980s gymnasium with space for two badminton courts and multiple markings for a range of indoor sports. On the nearside of the gym there are a couple of small tutorial rooms and a larger class-room used for a range of gym-based education courses. Adjacent to the large classroom is a weights and fitness area. The second gym on another part of the campus is smaller and provides machine, cardio and free weights equipment. Again, the environment is spartan and functional. It is reasonably well stocked even if the equipment is not brand new or state of the art. A range of activities are conducted in this gym. GP referral activities, health and wellbeing classes are carried out here, just as larger Olympic weights and bar-bells are available for body building and individualised strength and conditioning. There are no TVs, music, drinks machines or soft furnishings. Prisoners come here to train or participate on leadership or health-related courses.

Findings

Jack, Head of Reducing Reoffending, in charge of the Physical Education Instructors (PEIs) and their line manager, was clear that the diversionary, dis-ciplining elements of active sport participation are explicitly part of the prison's goals for prisoners. Jack stated that,

> I think there's no denying that the gym allows people to let off steam in a kind of healthy and productive manner, rather than many other ways that they could blow off steam.
>
> *(Jack, Head of Reducing Reoffending)*

Adding to comments in the focus group, Jack understands that some prisoners put great store in their access to physical activity in prison. The following Focus Group (FG) narratives are an indication of the value of gym access for prisoners.

> *FG response:* Keeps my mind clear. Stops me from getting a life sentence.
> *FG response:* That's what gets me by in jail. If I haven't got no gym … If you take the gym away from me, you might as well put me in the block and forget about me.

The gym facilities are granted to all prisoners as a basic requirement and dependent upon a prisoner's adherence to the prison rules, regulations and behaviour codes they will be awarded additional privileges of up to four sessions a week. Ken, an experienced PEI, illustrated this when he stated that,

> If you're on 'basic'… so you have been displaying negative behaviour over a prolonged period and you're downgraded to 'basic', you're not entitled to use

the gym on three of the four sessions. You would be able to attend, providing you're on the list, on the Friday afternoon.

(Ken, PEI)

Q: OK, so if I go down to the gym four times a week, 'I lift my weights, I go back to my room'… how is that helping me with rehabilitation?
FG *response:* So you don't kill someone … It keeps you away from drugs, from smoking, from come-backs. Stress relief. It just relaxes you or chills you.

There were some interesting contradictions that revolved around the efficacy of rehabilitation. The prison runs some education and community activity to help prisoners gain qualifications and experience before release. The prison runs basic leadership courses (levels 1–3) with a view to gaining the qualifications to become gym instructors. Strong candidates are also trusted to work with a community group that comes in once a week to use the hall. When asked about reoffending, Jack stated that,

As a service we don't actually record or target against that information any more. We used to own targets for releasing prisoners into employment, education, training and accommodation. We've handed over that target to the community rehabilitation company. So that kind of changes the focus slightly as well. And obviously lots of different people collect information about reducing reoffending, but it isn't something that as a service or as a prison we're given a certain figure for, and then kind of being able to measure any kind of change.

For the Head of Reducing Reoffending to not have a system to establish the impact of the interventions in the prison on individual prisoners means the prison can only draw on anecdotal evidence for the success of their rehabilitation activities.

Our access to prisoners finishes when they get released. So even when they go out on licence we still technically have no access to them, so although we can make referrals or have done some signposting, or even some hand-holding prior to release, at the end of the day once a prisoner is released we have no access to them anymore.

(Jack, Head of Reducing Reoffending)

The power of sport to rehabilitate is brought into question by the lack of evidence gathered and by some of the prisoner statements. Though a number of prisoners recognised the potential benefits of the leadership courses, a response from a prisoner in Focus Group 3 reinforced this point when he argued,

I don't see rehabilitation … I see that they've pulled us away from society and segregated us from innocent people, but what do they do to rehabilitate us? They do nothing.

Another prisoner concurred by saying,

> Yeah, but there's no-one sits here and goes … 'We'll support you'. No-one's ever sat there in my sentence and gone 'Right, why have you done what you've done? What do we need to do? What do I need to ask you?', or 'What do we need to do to stop you from doing it again?' Sport just covers about an hour or two of your day-to-day activities, and that's it.

Whether it is realistic to provide gym facilities and expect positive change has been questioned by numerous social commentators (Long and Sanderson 2001; Coalter 2007). With the prisoner pipeline link to resettlement in the community stopping on release, the prison is unable to maintain a feedback loop on prisoner issues, successes and failures. Reducing reoffending becomes an aspiration rather than an institutionally resourced system. As a result, the tensions for growing prison populations become compelling.

Prison service rules stipulate that,

> There must be equal access to PE programmes and resources to meet the requirements of all prisoners, through identifying and giving full considerations to meet specific needs of their gender, religion, age, disability, race, and sexual orientation. All those involved in delivering PE will recognise the diverse needs and abilities of those who use its services and give everyone an equal chance to develop and fulfil their potential […] PE departments will monitor equality of access to programmes, resources and outcomes by maintaining written evidence.
> *(Ministry of Justice/National Offender Management Service 2011: 6)*

However, like the aspirations for rehabilitation, the significance of ethnicity in terms of monitoring participation in the provision of physical education in the case study prison was not a priority. There was no ethnic monitoring on participation for the prisoners. The physical education instructors (PEIs) are stipulated by the Ministry of Justice's *PE for Prisoners* report (Ministry of Justice/National Offender Management Service 2011) to implement three key service outcomes. These are that (1) the physical health and wellbeing needs of prisoners are met, in part, through PE, (2) PE contributes to the safety, order and control within prisons, and (3) the life skills of prisoners are developed, in part, through PE. Prisoners over 21 years old must be given the opportunity for at least one hour of PE per week. Prisoners under 21 years old must have the opportunity to take part in at least two hours per week. The average attendance from *Prison PE Monthly* returns shows an average of 4.10 hours PE per week across the sector. In effect the basic privileges of prisoners are met, and where there are pressing needs concerning disability and health specific access or programmes have been implemented. 'Race' and ethnicity are not factors deemed by the prison or the PEIs to be of particular concern for attendance or any other matter. According to the PEIs they record general participation statistics,

We do record it, but we basically don't go into massive depth. We'll have the gym lists, for the recreational sessions, and of course we tick off people who attend and don't tick off people who don't attend.

(Mick, PEI)

I mean, we have a very broad spectrum in the gym anyway. Asian lads, black lads, white lads. You know, it's huge. But I don't know, it came down saying we don't have to do it anymore.

(Ken, PEI)

The explanation drawn from the group was blamed on bottom-line savings in the prison service. The relegation of a systematic ethnic monitoring process in the gyms meant a saving of PEI time and therefore a cutting back of resources for this prison. The same issues frustrated the Butler Trust (2014) workshops on 'Transforming Prisons and Prisoners through Physical Education'. Inconsistencies of approach to resourcing affected the quality and impact of PE provision across the sector.

About two years ago we went through something called benchmarking, and alongside that ran 'fair and sustainable'. Two huge reorganizational pieces of work. Basically, it was around saving money. It was all to do with the public sector and savings. So the two ran together. We got an amount of hours to deliver certain pieces of work. Lots of work was taken away at that time. Not just the monitoring stuff. Searching, all kinds of bits and pieces, in order to deliver a service that was cheaper.

(Brian, PEI)

As a result the observations from the PEIs concerning the significance of 'race' and representation were anecdotal reflections on their many years of being in the prison services. For example, this comment from Chris (PEI) refers to the changing ethnic representation over the years in prisons and how that has consequently made Black prisoners more conspicuous in the gyms,

If we did a little poll on it, we'd say 'Oh, there are too many Asians and black lads coming down.' They used to go 'Why aren't there any Asians or black lads?' Because there weren't as many Asian lads or black lads in prison when I first joined in 1988, whereas now they're over-represented.

(Chris PEI)

Mick (PEI) also stated,

There's no session where you think 'Oh, maybe we're not representing the ethnic minorities sufficiently.' At every session there's a large proportion, so there's no need …

Even though ethnic monitoring had been cut over the years in cost-saving exercises, the PEIs denied the relevance of 'race' in how prisoners mixed or 'associated' in the gym. Their collective view evoked a space where prisoners were more focused on their physical and social activities rather than exclusionary ingroup/ outgroup practices, as illustrated by Ken:

> You know, you could have four white lads training and they've got to make ... a black lad training with them. Or it could be the other way round, four black lads training with ... And you don't even bat an eyelid at all. And they don't bat an eyelid. Or you could have a group of Asian lads over there and a group of white lads over there. Next they'd be mixing and matching. I think because when they come to the gym they can do what they want. So they mix together ...

In Focus Group 1 the prisoners shared a similar view,

Q: Does race, ethnicity or religion make any difference?
ALL: No.
Q: Who do you socialise with?
PRISONER FG1: We're all together, us lot in here. We're all in tune with each other.

Field Group 3 had a similar response,

ALL: No. Not at all.
PRISONER FG3: No, because I train with Ginz, Stan. I wouldn't think ... I'd train with Jezz, or I'd train with him, or I'd train with him. It doesn't really matter about the colour of their skin as long as you're training together ...

Field Group 2 confirmed the view that 'race' was not an obvious structuring factor in how they participated in the gym and who they participated with. When asked *Have you seen any patterns of people training with each other because they're from a similar background? Ethnicity or religion or whatever?* The response was:

> Not really.
> No.
> Everyone knows each other in here.
>   If they know each other or if you're on the same wing and have got to know each other you train together.
>   Yeah, if they know each other.

Bonilla-Silva (2010) might argue that asking a group of people about their disposition to 'race' is likely to engender a response where racism or negative racial relations are *elsewhere*. In this case there was consensus across the three focus groups that 'race' was not a key organising factor in how they organised or experienced their activities in prison, nor was it perceived to be significant in how others associated. It was apparent that socially the prisoners were more instrumental about who they associated with and why. They were clear that the key criteria for inclusion into their groups were conviviality and mutual agendas: for example in Field Group 1 they noted that:

> We're on a non-smoking wing, us, so we bring the smoking cessation down. Friday or Monday, we can put a spinning class on, or an aerobics class. Half of them think it sounds g★★, but it isn't, it's good. They won't participate. 'I'm not doing an aerobics class, that's for women.' But it's good. So the lads who are decent lads, who want to train … It's better for us because there's only decent lads down here.
>
> You meet lads off other wings, you know, when they come down. They're on the same wavelength as yourself. Yeah, like, if we're training together, we'll plan a session together.
>
> No, I'm saying, none of us smokes [marijuana or spice], so you don't talk about 'give us a burn', because it's all about what you don't do and what you do do.
>
> There's always a saying 'if you hang about with smack heads, you'll be a smack head. If you hang about with somebody soft, you'll be soft.' So if you hang about with different individuals who have all got something different to bring to the table, we'll all get on with each other. Because you know when you're in the gym, it's like 'Yeah, yeah', and then when you go back to the wing you think 'F★★★ing hell, look at this lot here, what's going on.'

Conviviality and the shared health agenda of sport and PE aided the development of the bridging and bonding social capital across prisoners who at their core wanted to get through their sentence with as much of their identity and self-worth intact. Conviviality is emphasised in the way prisoners participate in sport, as those who do not meet the rules of engagement are excluded. This was revealed across all three prisoner focus groups by how they managed to best 'do their time' and with whom. They seemingly spent their gym time with others dependent on a mutual agenda of gaining maximum benefit from their gym privileges, regardless of biography. Catharsis, control, escape and wellbeing were crucial to the prisoners' ability to get to the end of their sentences with as little collateral damage to themselves as possible. The time that prisoners spend in their cells and in the institution is made more palatable by a gym environment that they feel in more control of, and happier in, than any other. Gym activities are a privilege and are therefore chosen by prisoners. On one level there is a level of agency in what a prisoner does with his association time and for many these privileges are crucial to building and maintaining a maximum number of sessions. Yet there is something about the gym environment that is different to other areas in the prison. The gym environment is the one area where they feel able to speak to officers on a first name basis, where officers are out of uniform, and where they can move freely from space to space as they socialise and do different activities. In an institution where everything else is about specific timings for specific activities framed by formal relations the gym environment brings a sense of relief and empowerment to prisoners.

FG1

If you ask all these gym staff, they're sound and decent with the lads, they talk to us on the level, not like officers, they engage different with us.

FG2

Q: Is it any different, though, generally, to the officers on the wings?

It's the same, innit?

I think it's different.

It's different because they're in a different situation, aren't they? If they were put in the gym and these lot were put on the wing, it would be different, wouldn't it?

You're not treated like a prisoner by this lot, you're just treated like anyone else in the gym. It's different.

FG3

It's more like they treat you like a person. Everywhere else, you're a prisoner. In here, you're more treated like a person. Obviously follow the rules, they treat you right, they give you a bit more freedom.

If you show them respect, they give you respect back.

It's more like normal society in here. No-one's stood over you watching what you do. They come in, they let you go do what you want to do, you can go from one room to the next with no-one saying 'where are you going?'

This sense of control cannot be underestimated in a prison context especially when 'doing time' for prisoners means getting through a day and being closer to the feelings of normality that they fleetingly get to remember and replicate in the gym environment. These opportunities in the prison are highly valued and recognised openly as such by the prisoners as control and escape mingle so for a while they are not in prison but could easily just be in a freely chosen gym in their community with some mates.

FG1

The training's an escape, innit? Because when you're in the gym you're not thinking about anything else. You just think about what you're doing.

It's something different, you get forward to it. You can plan your workouts, you can plan all sorts, your diet and your nutrition.

Q: … they're just trying to get out of jail for an hour, aren't they?

Definitely. Yes. Without that, we're banged up.

It takes you out of jail for one hour. You're not in jail. You're with your pals having a high-five, you're having a laugh and a joke, sharing whatever stories. And you're training hard. When you come out of the gym you think 'F***ing nice session, that. Nice one. See you tomorrow.'

It's like being at home with your mates, driving around in the car, it takes you out of here for an hour. It does me, anyway.

FG2

And it's a good release from your surroundings. It gets you away from your sur-roundings, what's happening on the wings and that.

FG3

So them sessions, you're looking forward to. Then when you stop going, you're looking forward to going back. It ticks away the time, so you're not counting days, you're counting gym sessions.

Like I was saying to you, when you come to the gym you feel normal. When you're on the wings you feel like a prisoner. When you're in the gym it's just like being in a gym on the outside.

It takes the jail away, it's not like you're in prison when you're in the gym, or when you're playing football in there or when you're playing whatever in there. It's not like you're in prison, you know.

In so far as sport in this prison is a tool of state control, the diversionary aspect of the gym environment is welcomed by the prisoners. There is a seeming win–win situation here as the disciplining element of sport and PE acting as a pressure valve, socialising instrument and diversionary technique is one of the most important factors to facilitate time passing in a way that is productive and on the terms of individual prisoners. Though the element of freedom in terms of choice, time and activity is highly limited, what the prisoners do with that time is personal and almost oasis-like in an otherwise highly controlled institution. As a result of the escapism of participation, the gym environment is highly significant for the pris-oners. Feelings of wellbeing emerge as prisoners talk of relieving stress, sleeping better, looking good and increasing confidence. From conversations with these prisoners, what is clear is the reduced significance of 'race' in how individuals experience their recreation. This observation is at odds with studies outside of prison contexts, and in this context contradicts studies on 'race' in sport and leisure.

Conclusion

As Richmond and Johnson (2009) found that we cannot ignore how 'race' affects the experience of prisoners, it is extended here to include the experience of prisoners and their sport. Where Meek et al. have explored the way prisoners experience sport in relation to ethnicity it is clear from the focus groups in this study that 'race' has a minor place in discussions of inclusion/exclusion, participation. Where Phillip (2000) argues that the benign nature of sport and leisure arenas can easily reinforce racial dynamics, it is also true that it can confound them where inclusivity is a product of prisoner proximity, convenience and social relations rather than ethnic differences. The seeming lack of distance across racial lines in this study is such a phenomenon (Du Bois 1994). While Du Bois (1994) argues about the perpetua-tion of colour lines, what seems more important for prisoners in this study is the sporting arena's potential for diversion rather than racial division (Brohm 1989). Goffman (1961) and Sabo (2001) argue that activities like sports that are relatively unserious help prisoners to serve their sentences better. Commonly referred to as 'doing time', these activities help to remove prisoners from their immediate circumstances,

> If the ordinary activities can be said to torture time, these activities mercifully kill it.
>
> *(Goffman 1961: 67)*

The idea of freedom as espoused by Norman (2015) is an essential element in the significance of sport and its potential to assist 'time to pass' in a productive and convivial way. Sport and PE are used to assert a level of control and disrupt the routine of the total institution. Goffman's (1961) reflections on self-determination through self-selected behaviour become much clearer at this point. The power of sporting contexts to facilitate connections with others was apparent as the prisoners bonded with like-minded others to help them 'do their time'. Part of this may also come from a sense of reconnecting to their 'pre-incarcerated selves', adjusting to incarceration (Goffman 1961). For the prisoners, there were sufficient conditions in place for the benefits of the sporting environment to include physical and mental health, social and psychological improvements, personal development and self-esteem, and positive relationship developments (Coalter 2007; Meek and Champion 2012). Though these are not properties of sport they remain part of the latent potential of the sporting arena, especially as others will choose to avoid sport for a range of other more or less productive or socially acceptable activities.

The significance of sport is made more serious when prisoners recognise that its normal function of counter-balance to the stresses and strains of civil society routines cannot be so easily controlled due to institutional convenience, access and time. The ideological values perpetuated by state provision of sport and PE opportunities linked to privileges and behaviour are transparent and clearly communicated. Part of the contradiction of sport and PE in prison is outlined by Sabo (2001), who juxtaposes the prisoners' desire for self-expression and physical freedom with the bureaucracy's desire to use sport to make prisoners more malleable and for purposes of social control. The dynamic of liberation and social control emphasises the instrumentality of sport as 'measured time' from different standpoints. Even as a 'prison of measured time', sport can bring relief, social and psychological gains, but at the same time it can reinforce disempowering rules while demoralising its targets. This function of sport as privilege or reward necessitates deeper explanation.

The hubris of sport stakeholders on the value of sport must be tempered by the impact of any removal or additional limitation of it for prisoners. Thus, any loss of access to the privilege of sport in a prison can be perceived to be more serious and harmful than on the outside. The rationalisation of the lives of these prisoners in the total institution of prison is such that many doubt their chances of adjusting outside of it. For some, their access to sport as a privilege of their incarceration is part of a jigsaw of complex tensions of work–play, sport–punishment, sport–reward, house rules, prisoner–staff, prisoner–prisoner. These dynamics make up part of a picture where sport has a part to play in managing time, demonstrating character and model identities, enacting symbolic control, catharsis and different forms of learning. Yet, half of the prisoners released reoffend within a year (Meek 2014). We also know that a disproportionate number of those incarcerated are Black and minoritised ethnic prisoners. If sport has a productive part to play in the way a prisoner manages his or her time it becomes extremely important to understand under what condition it works or otherwise (Long and Sanderson 2001; Coalter 2007). It is incumbent on all to be circumspect about the merits of sport for prisoners, though their voices are clear that a more specific comprehension of context, particularity, and meaning for prisoners and staff within the spaces of total institutions is required. Goffman (1961: 37) stated that,

> Socially distant persons find themselves developing mutual support and common counter-mores in opposition to a system that has forced them into intimacy and into a single, equalitarian [sic] community of fate.

Based on available research, Parker, Meek et al. (2014) were not unequivocal about how sport contributed to the experience of prisoners until they examined the impact of a specific education programme that incorporated sport. This multiagency approach to sport included personal support for prisoners through community and voluntary agencies. They argue that a comprehensive programme approach to sport in prison is likely to reveal positive outcomes socially, psychologically and in terms of rehabilitation. In the prison in the north of England where these focus groups took place the 26 per cent of the prisoners from a BME background are still heavily over-represented compared to approximately half that figure in the general population (ONS 2011). The increasing Black prison population is likely to benefit or be disadvantaged by what the prison system has to offer in regard to sport and PE. Though where BME prisoners are over-represented the potential for sport for this growing population is currently limited to managing their time rather than their rehabilitation back into society. In some ways the triage of prison services that include sport should focus more on the work of rehabilitation, especially in the knowledge that over half of released prisoners will be reincarcerated within a year. For the growing number of BAME prisoners and those from the dominant White population, it is clear that the potential of sport is being used in a limited but strategic way by both prisoners and prisons while the rehabilitation possibilities are poorly construed.

The racially organised prison politics that Richmond and Johnson (2009) argue is part of the underlife of prisons did not emerge here, though a larger study would further test this proposition across all categories of prison and not just one category C institution. Given the imbalanced ethnic population of prisons, future studies should focus specifically on the experiences of Black prisoners and their journey through the system. In the past the lack of ethnic monitoring in prisons has led to accusations of racial bias by prison staff that led to less sport and leisure time for Black prisoners. For the prison in this study, without its ethnic monitoring in place there is the potential for such negative patterns to occur (Coyle 2009). The relationship of Black prisoners to sport, prisons and other prisoners should be a central focus of ongoing research that moves on from considering prisoners as one group to acknowledging their diversity. In addition, for this to occur future research needs to be scaled up to include a range of all categories of prison, including those that host women residents.

Note

1 In prisons in England and Wales the terms sport, recreation, physical activity and PE are often used interchangeably. Physical education is more commonly used in policy to depict sport, physical activity and exercise. This reflects the nomenclature of those charged with managing the athletic function of prisons: physical education instructors (PEIs).

5

'RACE' AND CYBERSPACE

> While on stage at an awards ceremony in Shanghai on Friday, Williams was asked to
> explain his emotional reaction to a golfer's tournament win earlier this year – given
> that the caddie used to work for the former number one Woods. He told a room
> packed with leading golfers and tour officials, *I wanted to shove it up that black arsehole*.
>
> Huffington Post *(Sheriff 2011)*

Before Barack Obama entered the White House the notion of 'post-race' had
entered the lexicon of those excited by the World Wide Web and cyberspace.
Cyberspace is often viewed as a utopian or an ideal neutral space where 'race',
gender, age, religion and other social factors are washed out on a level playing
field. Nakamura (2002: xi) concurs that even 'transcending racism' was expected as
a likely outcome of the advent of the internet. However, she goes on to sensibly
argue that because we are not all equal in the world offline we are also unequal
online. It becomes salient to state that it is as important to focus our critical lens on
how 'race' and racism are played out in cyberspace, just as we have focused our
critical gaze more traditionally offline. Nakamura (2002) goes on to argue that,

> We continue to scrutinize the deployment of race online as well as the ways
> that Internet use can figure as a racialised practice if we are to realize the
> medium's potential as a vector for social change. There is no ignoring that the
> Internet can and does enable new and insidious forms of racism.
>
> *(Nakamura 2002: 30)*

This chapter explores how 'race' and racism are manifest and played out online in
what has been argued to be an egalitarian, 'post-race' space. It considers how those
online may feel less accountable to social norms and mores as they do when they
are offline. Offline their anonymous identities and protocols blur notions of
authenticity and acceptability in racialised debates. Hall (1998) holds the position

that modernist ideas of traditional processes of building arguments and opinion with others, rehearsing ideas, and developing consensus before publication are less relevant on the internet. As a consequence, extremism, bigotry and the perpetuation of racialised ideologies are more likely to be openly expressed.

In the UK, the equality and inclusion organisation Kick it Out promoted a new initiative to tackle episodes of discrimination on social media. Following rising incidents of abuse the campaign was used to raise awareness of abuse online, to recognise it, avoid it and report it. Kick it Out became conscious of the extent of abuse on social media after monitoring incidents over a season in the English Premier League. Governing bodies like those in football struggle to deal directly with online abuse because of the difficulties of being able to prove jurisdiction over the instigator of the specific sport-related abuse (Kick it Out 2016). During Euro 2016, Kick it Out analysed the problem further in relation to incidents arising from the 2016 European football championships, 'The Euros'. In the 2014/15 season it was estimated that there were over 134,000 instances of discriminatory abuse of which 95,000 were directed at Premier League clubs and 39,000 directly at Premier League players. In simple terms there was one abusive mention approximately every 2 minutes (Kick it Out 2016).

During the 2016 Euros from 10 June to 10 July 2016, 22,000 incidents of discrimination were recorded. Even though the Euros research included fans from across Europe the categories of abuse were consistent with the earlier research conducted by Kick it Out (Kick it Out 2016). From Table 5.1 it is clear that racism and sexism remain serious problems and prevail online as they do offline. Though these manifestations of racism and sexism are novel in the traditions of football bigotry they do not make them any more benign or less harmful (Bradbury, Amara et al. 2011; Bradbury, van Sterkenburg et al. 2015).

Kick it Out's concern with an unregulated internet is one shared by Whine (1997), whose view of the internet is to see it as a phenomenon that establishes sufficient conditions for discrimination to thrive. The relative lack of oversight on the internet makes him concerned that there is likely to be a steady increase in the

TABLE 5.1 Categories of online discrimination in European football

Types of discrimination over the 2014/15 English Premier League season: categories of abuse		Types of discrimination over the 2016 European Championships: categories of abuse	
Race	(28%)	Race	(28%)
Gender	(25%)	Gender	(27%)
Sexual orientation	(19%)	Disability	(22%)
Disability	(11%)	Sexual orientation	(13%)
Antisemitism	(9%)	Age	(5%)
Islamophobia	(5%)	Antisemitism	(3%)
Age	(2%)	Islamophobia	(2%)
Gender reassignment	(1%)	Gender reassignment	(0%)

Source: Kick it Out 2016.

amount of racist activity conducted and material available. For example, in Back's (2001) work on extreme Right groups he suggests that the notion of whiteness and the language that perpetuates it can propagate the notion of lineage, while the internet facilitates the perception of racial separation. Similarly, Cleland and Cashmore (2016: 29) found that dispositions to racism among football fans emerge from a mix of tastes, preferences and cognitive frameworks that regulate racial practices. Both Whine (1997) and Back (2001) agree that an unregulated internet presents ideal conditions for enabling and facilitating racists who can share ideas and information at will, and very quickly. Like most social arenas the internet is a site of struggle rather than a utopian, 'race'- and racism-free sanctuary (Leung 2005). So just as technologies like the internet can facilitate oppositional resources to empower and challenge racism then so can its alternative be envisioned through those technologies.

To do this the chapter takes a specific look at online responses to an article written by Associated Press journalist John Leicester (Leicester 2011) about an incident between Steve Williams (caddie) and previous world number 1 golfer Tiger Woods. This particular article was brought to my attention because it was one where my opinion was invited to establish whether Williams' words were indeed a racial slur or purely a matter of benign comments taken out of context. However, this chapter does not focus solely on the incident, nor primarily on the institution of golf, neither does it fix solely upon the raft of arguments that centre and decentre the racism in Williams' defence. Rather, it focuses on the dispositions that online commentators adopted to this incident, and views their responses as a nexus in which racial politics are constructed, defended, reiterated and resisted, making cyberspace *a point of negotiation between resistance and power* (Leung 2005 13).[1]

The study goes on to explore the responses to the Associated Press article by first offering a backdrop to golf's questionable history on race relations. Golf is one of the few sports to signal its racist intentions through its constitution, in keeping itself White or, as some of its key stakeholders might argue, *separate but equal*. The reputation of Tiger Woods is also considered as a factor in drawing forth the enthusiastic online comments. Woods is recognised as one of the greats of golf, with many arguing that he is *the* best golfer of all time and its most significant personality. He also attracts global attention as he has been the subject of much recent controversy after a long period of sublime ascendency. Woods has polarised his supporters while offering succour to those seeking headlines or who plain just don't like him!

Even with an African American president incumbent at the time of the incident, the significance of 'race' in the US, where Woods and Williams ply a lot of their trade, is still one of the most serious and pressing issues. W. E. B. Du Bois' warning that the colour line could be the most significant issue of the twentieth century has continued into twenty-first-century sport and occupies the minds of politicians, academics, activists and everyday folk in a continuous negotiation of power and resistance. In the words of Cornel West (2001), *Race Matters* and the words of Williams at the golf award ceremony where the incident took place could not be seen as an innocent comment in a world where blackness, 'race' and racism are replete with a negative history, ideologies and politics (Winant 2001).

Leung (2005) succinctly stated that blackness, especially in the way Williams used it in reference to Woods, refers to those who have been subjugated, discriminated against, and been subject in some countries to apartheid, slavery and economic exploitation. It is commonly held that the term 'black' is often used to unite those who have suffered racism and discrimination as a result of their colour, culture or minoritised background or status. In critical terms 'black' is more regularly used politically/collectively rather than descriptively. Thus it is fair to argue that Williams' use of the term black in this context was used in an everyday sense where 'In the vernacular, "race" is usually synonymous with "colour"' (Malik 1996 2). Though there are debates about how inclusive this term is for some social groups, its political, rather than descriptive, unifying qualities have emerged as a form of identification, empowerment and point of unifying resistance. Blackness as description is rarely seen as derogatory yet Williams' use of the defence that he was only describing the natural colour of Woods' *arsehole* seems highly disingenuous; its denigratory power comes from its history and cultural context. Blackness, as invoked by Steve Williams (quote above) is inextricably linked to 'race' and the necessary racial politics that it imbues, regardless of intent or motive. The impact and outcomes of such communications are therefore dependent upon the context and the clarity of the message.

Golf past, Tiger present

It would be remiss to consider Williams' utterances in isolation from the history of institutionalised racism in golf. Golf is not only a sport where racial disparities are as evident as in others, but it is a global sport that wrote into its constitution in 1943 that only White people could be members of its professional body, the Professional Golf Association (PGA). In many respects golf has not historically stopped at 'race' in seeking to remain an activity open to a select group of predominantly male, White, middle-class participants. In fact, the exclusion of Black golfers as professionals emerged from a discussion considering whether women should become registered with the profession. In 1943 a bylaw was adopted stating that players could only be members of the PGA if they were

> Professional golfers of the Caucasion[sic] race, over the age of eighteen years in North or South America, and who have served at least five years in the profession [...] shall be eligible for membership.
>
> *(Leonard 2000: 21)*

Golf has had many battles due to its penchant to maintain racism and sexism through segregation that has forced many unlikely candidates to challenge such dispositions. As a late convert and patron of golf, in 1952 Joe Louis, the African American boxer who battled Hitler's Nazi emissary and athlete Max Schmelling, chose to challenge the PGA because of its 'Caucasian only' rule. Louis, alongside other Black golfers, pressed the PGA over many years to include Black golf professionals in 'open' and 'invitational' competitions. Even after gaining concessions they found the few invitations they received still maintained the racially segregated practices that led to the racist microaggressions experienced through the (a) environment – separate facilities and segregated playing and playing times, (b) overt racism through the open hostilities of the 1950s pre-civil rights era, and (c) covert racism – the prejudices that consciously and unconsciously shrouded the playing experience of golfers at this time. Golf was clearly a reflection of its time and yet it did little to challenge the racism within. Where the 'separate but equal' principle was sanctioned in statutory instruments through Plessy v. Ferguson (1896), it was repealed by Brown v. Board of Education (1954) (Diette 2013). Yet professional golf, typified by its private sector, Whites only, elitist, male-centric institutions maintained its Whites only rule until the 1960s.

The PGA was comfortable endorsing this highly controversial approach even as Black people were being enlisted and fighting in World War II side by side with the very people they could not play golf with. This racist amendment was not deemed inappropriate until 1961, only 14 years before Tiger Woods was born. By this time generations of Black golfers had been more than disappointed by the institution of golf. Similarly, the careers of Howard Wheeler, Charlie Sifford, Teddy Rhodes and other talented golfers had been stymied by this engrained apartheid in golf. Leonard argues that one of the key reasons for the changes in 1961 emerged from a 1955 Supreme Court ruling against the City of Atlanta in the case between that city and Dr Holmes and his sons whose request to play on one of its municipal courses precipitated a skirmish to keep them out and a lawsuit to force their eligibility to play (Leonard 2000).

Even though Tiger Woods' biography follows him wherever he goes, in golf he is conspicuous by his blackness, which his sponsors and media have used to great effect. Starn's (2011) description of Tiger Woods' first television appearance at the tender age of two was unequivocally framed in a racial discourse. From the moment he entered the set of the Mike Douglas show with his father, and co-hosts Jimmy Stewart and the pro-celebrity golf icon comedian Bob Hope he was racialised and objectified by what seemed to be an adoring and awestruck public.

According to Forbes (Badenhausen 2012) Tiger Woods earned more for his sponsors in 2012 than world number 1 Rory McIlroy, even after a controversy-filled 3 years that spun his career out of control. Tiger is box office, big business because he is full of contradictions and promise. He is a husband who has fallen from grace with his wife. He is a father who has struggled to be a credit to his children. He is a fallen role model who still has the power to polarise opinions about golf's ability to include and exclude. Yet he is still viewed as a pioneer, one of the few Black golfers to become world class in a sport that has a history of excluding those who are not White, middle class and male. Tiger's ability to break through, become the most revered golfer of all time, forces a grudging recognition of greatness from whoever reads his record. Yet the thing that consistently sets him apart on most elite golf courses across the world is his blackness, not his maleness, not his fidelity, nor his integrity.

Apart from when he famously described himself as a Caucasian Black Indian Asian (Cablinasian), Woods has always been viewed as aloof and unwilling to discuss racialised issues, especially those of identity. In some ways it could be argued that he has used his immense wealth to cushion himself from the gritty realities of 'race' and the politics of 'race' that racialised celebrities are inevitably drawn into. Some Black celebrities such as Muhammad Ali, Tommie Smith and John Carlos, and Althea Gibson courted these debates openly while others like Tiger Woods skilfully avoided them. While he was able to play faultless golf and maintain a model 'race neutral' persona he was able to sidestep these issues as the business around Woods was also impeccable. While sponsors and the media were happy, Woods was able to ignore talk of his blackness, disengage with any political arguments in relation to it and seemingly transcend 'race'. However as Starn (2011: xvii) argues,

> The revelations about Tiger's serial infidelity – details like his seeming interest only in white women – reopened the matter of his racial identity in sometimes ugly ways. Suddenly, for example, Tiger's penis size became the object of much interest and speculation in the tradition of white fear, anxiety, and voyeurism surrounding the supposedly greater bedroom prowess of black men. This and much else about Tigergate showed an America angry, afraid, transfixed, curious, and resentful about racial politics in both old and new ways.

Woods once remarked of Orin Starn (Starn 2011) that professors should have better things to do than talk about him, and so at this point the chapter shifts from talking about Tiger Woods directly to now use an incident between him and his caddie Steve Williams as the context for this chapter on dispositions to 'race' and racism in cyberspace.

By not acting, golf flunks own racism test … ?

After Williams made his statement (above) the article syndicated around the world in September 2011 by the Associated Press (AP) sports columnist John Leicester provided the contextual background for this chapter (Leicester 2011). That piece was based on an incident that took place in Shanghai during which Steve Williams aimed a racial slur against Tiger Woods. In his article, entitled 'By Not Acting, Golf Flunks Own Racism Test', Leicester argues that failure to take action against Steve Williams for his racially motivated utterances makes a mockery of the PGA's grandiose claims that the sport promotes zero tolerance of racism. In addition, the article attacks the many senior golf personalities who witnessed this event but still refrained from speaking out to reprimand Williams. John Leicester concludes that golf's rhetoric of zero tolerance has been decisively found wanting.

Leicester included observations of the timid institutional response of the PGA. The joint statement of the PGA tour commissioner Tim Finchem and European Tour chief executive George O'Grady drew much criticism from those disappointed by the sport's response to Williams' words. The two men said they spoke for the PGA when they stated,

> [the PGA] feels strongly there is no place for any form of racism in ours or any other sport. We consider the remarks of Steve Williams, as reported, entirely unacceptable in whatever context [...]. We are aware that he has apologized fully and we trust we will not hear [such] remarks ever again. Based on this, we consider the matter closed, and we will have no further comment.
>
> *(Ferguson 2011)*

Analysing online sources

Within hours of the Associated Press article appearing, over seventy online responses were received in reaction to the article. The responses were diverse in terms of their stand on the incident, as some supported the tenor of Leicester's argument, yet others opposed the tone of the article. It is these responses in particular that this chapter explores because of the relative antisocial disposition of the online commentators' tone that veered from complete ambivalence to open racial hostility. The seventy-plus online respondents were identifiable only through their arbitrary user names and did not provide any socio-biographic attributes that could help identify them more adequately, such as real names, gender, age, place of residence, ethnicity, and so on. Notwithstanding this unavoidable limitation, this study set out to organise, describe, and analyse the pattern of dispositions and politics that the respondents portrayed toward 'race' and racism in sport, using their comments as the only unit of analysis.

It was found that there was a tendency for respondents to deny or trivialise the incident which took a wide range of patterns. The overriding motive was to challenge and undermine the racial characterisation of the incident by emphasising its insignificance and therefore encouraging others to do the same. The key distinction is that the category of *denial* refers to the view that claims racism did not occur, and *trivialisation* moves to undermine, mock, or ignore the significance or consequence of racism. They are also indicators of the small step from racial ambivalence to racism and race hate speech.

There are few studies focused on the internet, 'race' and racism and yet the influence of the internet on our lives is such that it is a missed opportunity for many social researchers. Silver (2000) argues that social factors such as 'race', gender and age have been given little attention in the cyberculture literature. He suggests that web entrepreneurs have shown more interest than academics due to the desire to understand the demographics of markets and therefore generate intelligence to pitch new products (Foxton 2012).[2] This relative invisibility leads Nakamura (2002) to describe it as the online raced body being 'outed' by commercial forces.

Silver suggests that the few signifiers of identity that people use on the internet generally ignore 'race', whereas gender is at least implicit (if not 100 per cent reliable) from a name or even pseudonym.

Other social factors such as age or sexual orientation are also regularly absent, and yet in a debate about racism the lack of biographical data, especially in relation to ethnicity, makes the assumptions and assessment of text and the meaning behind those texts precarious. Difficulties are likely to arise when conclusions are drawn about statements on the internet that themselves reinforce racial stereotypes and discourses. For example, an insightful critical and emotional challenge to racial slurs on the internet by anonymous individuals cannot be reduced to the episteme of those Black and or minoritised groups in society as this reductionism has no place in the politics of antiracism. Offline interactions reveal many signifiers of social characteristics and biographies to help researchers contextualise responses that often remain unspoken or ambiguous online in chat rooms, blogs and even tweets. Given all of the fallacies, anomalies and paradoxes of 'race' illuminated by eminent scholars, its common focus is constructed with reference to tangible, physical beings.

Unlike the internet, television is categorised as a 'push' medium due to the communal, shared but minimal interactivity element of this consumption (Leung 2005). There is minimum interactivity because the communication is generally one-way. The internet as a 'pull' media is necessarily individualised/isolated and interactive. In many cases lone computer users interact with uncurated/unregulated text, beyond a few peer review processes where users can report offensive material. The internet, and in particular online responses, can be as intellectually informed, humorous, reflective or unbiased as its users wish. The context in which users interact with the internet is such that without a physical social milieu in close proximity many are less politic and reflexive, and therefore it can facilitate unguarded and impulsive responses. Some of the online responses to the Associated Press article are examples of speech that offline may have been subject to more consideration and self-censorship.

'Race' in internet analysis

The online responders in this study appeared to display signifiers of whiteness as far as could be reasonably determined. However, this leads to a methodological word of caution. In drawing such conclusions there is the danger that researchers of 'race' may fall into the same traps that they wish to disrupt themselves; they should not draw upon the reductionist tenets that they wish to challenge. Physical identification is imperative to piecing together the logic and rationality of arguments on 'race' (Burkhalter 1999: 60). Signification of experience and understanding is read into debates and statements that online anonymous views generally do not volunteer. To a certain extent, verbal and physical cues are often acknowledged as de facto *convincers* or free floating signifiers in arguments where claims to knowledge on social issues are asserted.

However, Kang (2003: 39) takes this analysis further by arguing that 'race' can be socially constructed and reified online through a form of 'racial mechanics'. Three elements interact as individuals *map* (rules used to classify people into categories: physical or discursive signals) others into preconceived *racial categories* (through which basic concepts of race are understood) that stimulate *racial meanings* (cognitive beliefs about and affective reactions to the categories) for the user. This racial schema operates well at the level of understanding how 'race' is constructed as the paradoxical 'presence' of 'race' in the thinking and behaviour of individuals leading to racialised assumptions and dispositions about themselves and others. Online commentators' reactions to each other, and researchers' interpretations of comments, can all fail due to reductionist ideologies in assuming biographies, especially where text is the only form of communication. Even when a comment is carefully and insightfully crafted, without the author's corroborated offline identity or verification there remains an unnerving unease about the nuances of content. The background and experience of the speaker remains in doubt when this happens and so their words can lose some of their gravitas and authority at least in the first instance, significantly because *the body is synonymous with identity* (Donath 1999: 29).

The analysis of the social location, values and disposition of the respondents in these online responses drew on Goffman's (1959: 14) idea of 'expressions given' and 'expressions given off'. The former are the deliberately stated messages signifying how one would like to be perceived while the latter are more subtle and sometimes unintentional messages communicated via nuance or act. Though Goffman does warn that expressions given off can be communicated deceitfully or even feigned, Nakamura (2002) describes this as cybertourism as identities are donned without any consequences offline. Donath (1999) is sensible in stating that it is hard to maintain a persona or social characteristics that are not yours/or your experiences without eventually being found out, especially by those with real experience of being from specific social backgrounds. Key considerations in this study involved how to recognise authenticity in terms of identities, sincerity and insight, based upon the text through the information given, and given off by those commentators most aggrieved in their opposition to the Associated Press view that Williams committed a racist act.

Trivialisation and denial online

A propensity to trivialise the racialised harm in Williams' words became clear in the online responses to the article by Leicester (2011). There were also rhetorical devices used to minimise the significance and impact of racism in this case. Trivialisation emerged through semantic turns, sarcasm and pedantic arguments as the complexities of 'race' and racial politics were simplified to render them impotent and benign. Trivialisation is closely connected to the phenomenon of denial, and some comments were both trivialising and in denial of racism simultaneously (Bonilla-Silva 2006; Feagin 2010). The key distinction is that trivialisation politics resists the effects of racism by moving to undermine or mock, its significance or consequences.

Denial refers to the view that racism did not occur, or that 'that's not racism' was merely reference to the lesser evil of a 'racial slur'. A large segment of the proponents of trivialisation also utilised a simplistic rhetoric to insist that blackness and whiteness are neutral, non-political descriptors in order to undermine the claim that the incident was manifestly racist. As in the case of denial, trivialisation also materialised through the use of anti-political correctness rhetoric as a tool to divert and even subvert the substantive discourse focusing on the claims of racial discrimination embedded within the article. Consider the following examples:

> the comment was vulgar, but not racist. He called him black and last time I looked 'black' was not a racist term.
>
> *[Don]*

This comment presents multiple readings as it employs a semantic argument spliced with sarcasm to decentre blackness and its deployment by Williams. It combines the politics of denial through trivialisation while holding to a simplistic argument that could appeal to some as 'commonsense' and therefore be worthy of consideration. Another commentator [Ted] weighs in as follows:

> what's racist about it? If Williams said … WHITE @#$%, would that be racist?

Like [Don]'s, this comment is also complex and multipronged in its politics, though to be clear, if Woods had said this about Williams it would still have been a racial slur. Here, [Don] deploys rhetorical questions to spin the argument that the word 'black' in this context cannot be racist, admonishes the journalist for being ignorant, and dismisses the claims of racial discrimination to achieve an emphatic withering conclusion. For Feagin (2010) this attempt at sarcasm would suggest the deployment of an anti-black racial frame through the invocation of the possibility of an anti-white racial frame. However, there remains a lack of resonance in such false indignation as the power of the Williams statement has severe ramifications through an established anti-black ideology that is not present in an anti-white frame.

The turn employed by [Don] also invalidates the asymmetrical impacts of racism on Black and White recipients. Among others, the same kind of trivialising politics and rhetoric is portrayed by [Jerry] who wonders:

> I must have missed something. Is Tiger's @$$hole actually not black? Is it white?

Still, some of the comments in this category seem to combine trivialisation with mockery and satire. For instance, [Dave] maintained that there is

> so much uproar over so little. Tiger is an @#$% and was called out on it

whereas another respondent mocked the incident saying

> Waaaaaaaaa, the mean man hurted ma' black feelins'!
>
> [McBold]

Here the trope of a stereotypical, immature, yet ignorant black patois is invoked in this consciously inflammatory comment. This comment would not look out of place on one of the five websites that Weaver (2011) examined for racist jokes. The comment is powerful because of its willingness to reinstate and represent the racialised vernacular while also suggesting that only a childlike individual could be hurt by such a statement. Neither is this any child either, it is specifically a Black child, which therefore trivialises the uproar further and simultaneously demeans anyone who might have taken offence.

Privilege online

Proponents of denial and trivialisation are also historically located within a position of privilege and therefore their politics have a propensity to ignore or undermine racist experiences. Mills (2007) has famously described this as 'white ignorance' where the interests of whiteness are maintained through a complex array of devices and turns, one of which is the practice of ignoring major racialised issues. In the online responses this was manifest in discussions reduced to the fundamental differences based on phenotypic properties such as the colour of Tiger Woods' skin. The central thrust of these apolitical approaches represents an unproblematic project to de-politicise blackness (and whiteness) and 'race'. Attempts to lessen the impact of the comments by Williams were demonstrated by commentators seeing blackness as purely descriptive of skin colour and therefore a trivial neutral social characteristic; much like height or weight. Striking examples of such comments were found in attempts to destabilise claims of racism based purely on the simplistic notion that the 'black' in 'black arsehole' was purely descriptive rather than making reference to Woods' racialised social and cultural location and the politics of 'race'. To these commentators, Tiger's 'blackness' is deployed as a matter-of-fact rather than as a racially loaded reference.

Other more socially aware online responders' use of the terms 'black' or 'white' recognised the operation of 'race', racism or racial discrimination. For example, [David S] maintained that

> if he wouldn't have said 'black' it would have been okay.

Another respondent called [Skweeze] raises similar concerns when he observes that

> there are all sorts of things this guy could have said about Tiger without referring to his colour or his race ... the guy was wrong and the remark was very racist.

Both [David S] and [Skweeze]'s politics, which may be correct in this specific context, are that the muting of the term 'black' in discussions or references involving Black people can still result in uncivil but covert racially loaded interactions to reduce perceptions of racism. This indeed was the starting point for many of the discussions in this debate.

In sum, many of the online responses in this study take an overly simplistic view of the significance of 'race' and racism seemingly based on intuitive versions of the concepts, adopting perspectives that minimise the presence, significance and impacts of racisms. The complexity and subtlety of the ways 'blackness' and 'whiteness' are used in wider society are ignored in this trail of responses to effectively reduce them to benign descriptive terms. Here the online responses demonstrate the power of internet users to raise and defend racialised issues and relations in an open and relatively uncontested fashion. The fundamental premise of online responders who embraced apolitical views is that by defending Williams (and therefore themselves) by saying he only described Tiger Woods in terms of his skin colour, they present a clear rationale for not seeing any negative racialised slur.

When racism isn't

Though there are many sociological descriptions of racism that cover individual, institutional and structural processes and practices, it is important to stress that there are variegated forms of racism and therefore definitions. In Chapter 1 Anthias and Yuval-Davis (1993: 2) refer to 'racisms' to reflect this complex concept as noun, adjective and verb. A strand of semantic rhetoric was deployed by some respondents aimed at trying to establish a significant and exclusive distinction between 'racism' and a 'racial slur' and hence to problematise and cloud the correct characterisation of Steve Williams' alleged racist remarks. Proponents of this semantic fallacy appeared satisfied to concede that the remark could be 'rude', 'distasteful' and a 'racial' slur; but many firmly insisted the remark was not an act of racism. From the perspective of the online responders' constructions, the act of being called a racist is worse than the behaviour. [Hotnuke] argues

> No, Mr. Leicester, now we know the vast majority of those in sports media don't know the definition of a RACIAL SLUR. You're a pathetic idiot.

[Ultra-Humanite] and [Hilltopper] were also keen to agree with [Hotnuke] as they argued that,

> Uhhh while his comments were distasteful and clearly he is a jerk, I'm not sure where this racist angle comes from. Perhaps people should actually understand the words they throw around in columns they write. Just because you have an opinion, doesn't mean it can't be wrong.
>
> *[Ultra-Humanite]*

The commentators captured this semantic shift and exploited it as a tool for denying the occurrence of racism and problematising its characterisation. The underlying rationale for some seemed to be that a 'racial slur' is less harmful and can therefore be more easily conceded than 'racism'. In entrenching this line of argument, the commentators also repeatedly criticised the media and Associated Press for their perceived ignorance and narrow political correctness. [Hilltopper] was also happy to personalise the response to the AP journalist when remarking,

> Another writer with a fifth grade ability. Find a decent writer if you are going to cite racism in golf. Williams remark wasn't racist you idiot!
>
> *[Hilltopper]*

One respondent [SupplyChain99] went further to provide a definition of racism to emphasise the core arguments of this claim:

> Definition of racism: a belief that race is the primary determinant of human traits and capacities and that racial differences produce an inherent superiority of a particular race. By definition, his comments were not racist. Rude, dumb and hateful? Yes! Racist?

[SupplyChain99]'s pedantic assertion that this one, uncontextualised definition of racism encapsulates all forms of racism is convenient and reflective of broader commonsense views that racism is easily defined and perhaps made overly complex by those who purport to be affected by it. However, he does not explain why Williams' comments are 'rude', 'dumb' or 'hateful'. One could say this is an admission of racism without speaking its name. Though [SupplyChain99] does not engage a more complex view of racisms he 'gives off' more information about himself and his own experience and understanding of racism than anything else. Such a narrow view of racism is not likely to be held by one who has experienced it or has insight to these issues. In sum, defending Williams' motives are not the point here because as Bonilla-Silva (2006) argues, *you can't have racism without racists.*[3] Williams may not have done something like this in the past nor have done it since but it could be argued that what should be of concern here is the racial slur and its subsequent impact.

Interestingly [Mr. Southmetroatl], who appeared to be a Black American, also weighed in with arguments that concede that a racial slur occurred in this instance and denied any outright racist wrongdoing … before then accusing Steve Williams of possibly being a racist(!).

> Williams made a comment that most any person on the planet would have made, provided they know the English language and American vulgarities … I've traveled the world over and in every country I've been, the 'N' word is known throughout, and the natives know how to use it. When they used it toward me, I gave them pure American defensive flavor as ugly as they know

we can be. This is a tough world and regardless of color we'd better know how to handle ourselves in every situation … The comment was a racial slur but not an act of racism … though it might indicate this big-mouth might be racist. That's his business.

[Mr. Southmetroatl]

[Mr. Southmetroatl] attempts to inject a semantic distinction between 'racism' and 'racial slur', not to trivialise the significance of the issue but perhaps to lessen the premeditated conscious knowledge of the act perpetrated by Williams in Shanghai and the subsequent PGA response. Note that he does not try to minimise the potential of Williams' racist attitude, he is purely unclear of the direct relationship between racial slurs and racism. However, as someone who has had to defend himself against the 'N' word at home and abroad he appears to suggest that he is certainly not speaking from a position of White privilege, nor is he employing the politics of trivialisation. [Mr. Southmetroatl] found it necessary to 'give' some biographical information about himself to qualify the authority of his testimony. As in the offline world, the same problems of ethnic identities and identification remain part of a dynamic struggle between the structure of online media and the agency of individual interactants. Young (2001) argues that far from the utopian vision of erasing 'race' the internet has become a source of frustration for many Black and minoritised ethnic people who have protested at the default whiteness of cyberspace. E-'raced' users have had the double problem of feeling the need to state their racialised identities in conversations while risking being accused of bringing 'race' into everything. Nakamura (2002) asserts that,

> Though it is true that users' physical bodies are hidden from other users, race has a way of asserting its presence.
>
> *(Nakamura 2002: 31)*

[Mr. Southmetroatl] adopts a pragmatic realist standpoint, explaining that racial abuses are inevitable and commonplace occurrences, and challenges Black people to toughen up and deal with the everyday reality of it. However, this life lesson takes a different strategic political tone to those online responders who off-handedly announced that those offended by Williams' comments and the response of the golf authorities should *just get over it*.

OK … but … get over it!

The second pattern of denial entails the unilateral appeal by some online responders for readers to rise above this minor incident and move on with the more important affairs of their lives. Those who adopted this reasoning either denied any racist wrongdoing outright, or implicitly conceded racism occurred but advocate that people should just 'get over it'. [Edward] claimed as follows:

> If someone stood up there and said the same thing about my 'skinny white @#$%' (and if he where black) I'd laugh that little thing off right then and there. This crap just fuels hatred between the races.

Here, not only is Edward choosing to deny the salience of racial subordination of Black people by suggesting that verbal assaults can be laughed away, but he is also suggesting that those who invoke the idea of racism in this case are themselves racist. He gives us insight into his White identity, which lessens the authority of the advice given to those who critically sympathise or can empathise with experiences of racism. This minimisation of racism's effects is one that Bonilla-Silva argues is a central frame of colourblind racism where Black and minoritised ethnic groups are accused of using 'race' to their own ends. The 'race card' is a term sometimes used at these junctures.[4] [Detroit's Finest] also argues:

> how is it racist? Tiger is black right? So him saying he was trying to shove it up tigers [sic] black arse is racist? My assistant is black and she says they can kiss my black butt all the time. That is not a slur.

[Detroit's Finest] chooses to ignore the racial and semantic dynamics in this case. The conflation of issues and contexts here is one that is a privilege of one who has learned to evade exploring the significance of such nuances and proceeds to maintain his acceptance of this practice of ignorance. In addition to reinforcing a Black–White binary and racial difference, these comments portray a discourse of the privileged and can be interpreted within the broader context of the social location enjoyed by whiteness and the privilege of not suffering past racism. In fact, just like [Don] earlier, it is also connected to his apparent awareness that such a reference to his 'white arse' is either extremely unlikely to occur or would nevertheless be far less harmful to him. Put differently, this commentator has no direct way of knowing, nor wishes to understand, what a Black or minoritised person would experience in a similar situation.

Not having suffered victimhood with regard to racism therefore would make it relatively easier for some to trivialise or deny racism and to construct it as an unimportant phenomenon and therefore urge people to simply ignore it. [Sipp], for example, remorselessly tells readers to

> give it a rest … It is over, done, finished.

Another commentator, [Bad Service] goes further and proclaims

> Enough already with all this Race card stuff. Everyone has issues. Whites are now the minority so get over it people!

[Aaron], a respondent well entrenched in this thinking, rubs in the denial rhetoric using a version of what Bonilla-Silva would describe as the 'abstract liberalism' that contributes to colourblindness:

I am all for equality, but it is a joke listening to these righteous phonies … Get a life and quit squabbling over every small comment or anything resembling a joke, We need a tougher society.

Conclusion

The contention that the internet is the last frontier of social equality is presented with a sizeable challenge here. 'Race' and racism are seen to be constructed and challenged without anxiety during the course of the online exchanges following Steve Williams' comments in Shanghai. The tenor of the discussion reinforces the salience of 'race' in online *and* offline society, emphasised by how 'race' was unproblematically constructed and discussed in this online space. The everyday nature of this debate belies the suggestion that cyberspace is the last colourblind, 'race'-neutral, level playing field. In many ways this view ignores the notion that those Black and minoritised groups that have been regularly subject to racialisation and racism come to the internet *already marginalised, fragmented and imbricated within systems of signification that frame them in multiple and often contradictory ways* (Nakamura 2002: xvi).

Feagin (2010) suggests that a lot of racism occurs in the spaces where White people feel that the subjects of their racist behaviour are not likely to be. Feagin calls this the 'backstage'. One example is Steve Williams' behaviour at the private caddies' evening; given the demographics of golf, this could be described as one such occasion. Another one is the online space inhabited by the seventy-three online responses to John Leicester's Associated Press article. The pressures to adhere to the norms of politeness and sociability are often skewed in such situations where perceptions of similarity and 'insiderness' facilitate a relaxing of social norms; visible outsiders are more likely to make such situations 'uncomfortable'. The implicit whiteness of the internet also facilitates a different kind of backstage arena for many willing to act upon a racially biased ideology. Through the seeming privacy of the internet, its individualistic communications process and the relative anonymity of the interactants, cyberspace becomes a 'safe space' for normally borderline and abhorrent views.

The strategic denial of the implicit racism of Williams' comments by himself, the online responders and the Professional Golf Association is symbolic of the easy communication of dominant racialised values across real and virtual spaces. Turns to trivialisation and denial, through semantics, ambivalence, humour, mockery and practices of ignorance leave no doubt that cyberspace is clearly racialised, though sociology's understanding of these racial dynamics remains under-developed. Though not the focus of this study, a point for critical examination must be that as a site of struggle the internet must be seen as a vehicle for racisms to be propagated, though the corollary of this is that it must also be seen as a point of resistance. The strength of denial and trivialisation of racism in this case is clear. The nature of the multifarious rhetorical turns to achieve these standpoints in the online responses to the Associated Press article reflects patterns of behaviour that maintain racialised relations. These patterns, underpinned by a mixture of racial ideologies and the learned ignorance that perpetuates them lead to cyberspace remaining a contested space. The notion of a post-race utopia leaves many sceptical; hence I concur with Nakamura's (2002) call for researchers to maintain a critical gaze on 'race' and how it plays out on the internet.

Notes

1 Though not the focus of this chapter, it could also be argued that the associated reference to sodomy in a predominantly male space by Williams suggests the reinforcement of a disempowering hegemonic heteronormativity and homophobia. This element of Williams' utterances was missed by the media and in particular golf's governing body, the PGA. This is instructive in terms of the institutional recognition of oppressions that invariably intersect while perpetuating a hierarchy of issues. Patriarchy and heteronormativity remain intact due to societal fears of being labelled racist, while the focus on sexism and homophobia are marginalised and ignored in these predominantly male spaces.
2 Recent accusations of racial profiling against Google are indicative of such interests.
3 Bonilla-Silva refers to individuals, groups and entities such as governing bodies or other institutions.
4 The recent suggestion that racism on the pitch should end with a handshake at the end of the game by Sepp Blatter (then FIFA Chief Executive) is another such instance.

6

HUMOUR AS RESISTANCE IN STORIES OF RACISM

One of the nice perks that comes with these lecture "gigs" is a decent hotel. This one was no exception. My accommodation were on the hotel's VIP floor equipped with special elevator access key and private lounge on the top floor overlooking the city. As I stepped off the elevator, I decided to go into the VIP lounge, read the newspaper, and have a drink. I arrived early, just before the happy hour, and no one else was in the lounge. I took a seat on one of the couches and began catching up on the day's news. Shortly after I sat down comfortably with my newspaper, a White man peeked his head into the lounge, looked at me sitting there in my best (and conservative) "dress for success" outfit and high heels and all and said with a pronounced Southern accent, "What time are y'all gonna be servin'?": I tell this story both because story-telling is a part of critical race theory and because this particular story underscores an important point within the critical race theoretical paradigm, i.e. race [still] matters.

Gloria Ladson-Billings (1998)

This chapter builds upon the way critical race scholars have examined critical behaviours and phenomena of resistance. Some of them include the dynamics of interest convergence (Bell 1980; Gillborn 2009), the performance of antiracism (Ahmed 2006), liberal meritocracies and colourblindness (Bonilla-Silva 2010), and the operation of everyday microaggressions (Sue 2010). Processes of racial profiling and desistance (Glover 2009; Glynn 2014) and the implications of counter-storytelling (Yosso 2005; Aleman and Aleman 2016) also hint at a small number of the fault lines in activist scholarship. The use of humour in storytelling is part of a story of resistance that has not been explored in sport.

Humour is found in all social settings, though significantly for Lockyer and Pickering (2005) it is not synonymous with comedy and joke telling. Humour has been viewed as a way to ridicule and disempower in a range of fashions. On the other hand, humour in stories offers opportunities to empower and liberate oneself from problems and oppression (Bowers 2005). For example, Robidoux's (2004; 2012) study of the Kanai

First Nations ice hockey team in Canada revealed how stories and the humour within can disrupt the power of racism and historical colonisation (see also Gunn Allen 1992; Vizenor 1994), and in literature viewed as a way to contend with the tragic (Gaggiano 2005). Watson (2015) goes so far as to say that the subtleties of humour are significant in the human experience and that we ignore its effects at our peril.

Where humour has been explored in research it has focused on its ambiguities and qualities and mainly joke telling, though its use as a technique to resist racial ills is unclear. It is argued here that humour can be used to handle and disrupt unpalatable experiences of racism. Such techniques facilitate the sharing of cultural wealth which typically informs the cultural capital to navigate and resist negative experiences (Yosso 2005). Though racism and racial humour have been evidenced as pernicious aspects of sport, the use of racialised humour as offence and defence is complex and requires further examination.

The chapter aims to explore how humour techniques work to resist the impact of racism, and in order to capture this the research has revolved around three main questions: (1) How is humour used by Black coaches as a technique in stories of sporting oppression? (2) How does humour challenge their negative experiences of racialisation in sport? And (3) What do their stories of racism tell us about sport? Rather than an analysis of racist humour, this chapter enlivens the debate on how humour can work to console/include and deflect/exclude for Black and minoritised coaches in sport. The chapter begins with a consideration of how humour has been incorporated in the sport literature. It then moves on to outline key theoretical themes drawn from humour studies that underpin the critical race approach adopted here. Following this, the methodology becomes the precursor to a critical presentation of the findings from a focus group of Black football coaches in England and their stories of racism in football. The conclusion draws out how humour can be recognised in storytelling and how it can strategically empower the voices of Black coaches.

This chapter is not used to specifically define humour or what is funny, which Ostrower (2015: 184) suggests is experienced when intellect (wit); emotion (levity or gaiety); and physiology (laughter or smiling) coalesce; rather it illustrates signs of humour in how Black coaches recount racialised events (Andronoviene 2014). These signs of humour are more than joke telling and anecdotes about funny events but stories that apply the strategic use of humour in ordinary everyday events. Humour in the context of everyday racism in sport emphasises Delgado's notion of *humus*, the supposed root word for 'humour', *to bring racism low and down to earth* (Delgado 1995: 61). By focusing on everyday racism in football/sport the chapter further reveals (a) the way it directly affects Black and minoritised individuals, (b) racism's variegated forms, and (c) strategies used to lessen or disrupt racism's impacts.

Sport and humour

Though Snyder (1991) lamented the relative lack of interest in sport and humour, there still does not seem to have been a significant shift in its allure (Snyder 1991). The literature on sport and humour is scant, and what has been written has emphasised more overt and predicable themes that include the place of jokes and banter (Snyder 1991; Burdsey 2011), sexism and gender (Shaw 2006; Anderson 2015), and sport cultures and team cohesion (Sullivan 2013). Where humour has been explored in relation to racism in sport there has been an insightful focus on the mitigation of racism and bigotry as jokes or disparagement and superiority (King 2006; Burdsey 2011; Reid 2015).

Snyder (1991) argued that humour in sport has the potential to reveal previously unexplored phenomena. He revealed the commonalities in descriptions of humour that had at their core types of discontinuity or incongruity that suggest more than one way to read an event. For Snyder (1991), what makes something humorous is to describe a scene so that the audience understands the alternative reading(s) and 'get it' in what Snyder (1991: 119) describes as a *resolution of conflicting images*. Like Sullivan's (2013) analysis of sociable traits in teams, Snyder also considered playful behaviour when he considered how humour could be used as building blocks for sport team cohesion. Similar to Anderson's (2015) criticism of sexism and gender in sport, he also explored humour as superiority and disparagement. Where humour has been explored in relation to sport, themes that examine team dynamics and character traits (Sullivan 2013), sexism and gender relations in sport cultures are popular topics (Shaw 2006; Anderson 2015).

In Reid's case, humour was examined to explain how it could be used to deny intolerance or justify the discriminatory comments about the sectarianism of the Celts and the Irish. King (2006) had similar concerns about the Anti-Asian (American) racism in sport. Though not the focus of this chapter, in both Reid (2015) and King's (2006) work, racist perpetrator(s) have attempted to lessen the impact of their actions by trivialising them as humour. Consequently, Clarke (1998) argues that jokes can act as the 'velvet glove' of racism, as they perpetuate previously unpalatable myths in a more acceptable way in what Ford et al. (2015) term 'disparagement humour'. Contrary to this chapter, Snyder (1991), as with the other studies of sport and humour mentioned thus far, focused primarily on events that were deemed to be humorous that would then enable a critique to explain why they were problematic, or viewed as such.

In addition, this chapter builds on Burdsey's (2011) work that illustrates how racism in sport is manifest through a plethora of racial microaggressions in the everyday. Microaggressions that emerge through personal, institutional and environmental factors; microinsults, microassaults and microinvalidations (see Sue 2010). Burdsey's (2011) concern with the place of humour in masking the presence of racism in sport emerges from a need for those in sport to move beyond common conceptions of racism and discrimination in sport as being things of the past. The consequence of adopting such a passive stance is to allow racism to thrive, unfettered and unchallenged.

Theories of humour

Bowers (2005) describes using humour as a form of communication that can have the effect of (i) an ethnic glue, (ii) a celebration of survival, and (iii) a release of intercultural and interracial tensions. Similarly, Wilkins and Eisenbraun (2009) summarise the physiological uses of humour as a coping mechanism. In relation to extricating something light out of stressful situations, Wilkins and Eisenbraun (2009) argue that through humour everyday struggles and disappointments become easier to manage and overcome. Humour is also seen as a way to speak truth to power (Andronoviene 2014) or to shift situations from the negative to the positive. Weaver (2011: 27) considers the shifting of negative to positive using a technique of reversing the negative effects of racism. Yet he goes on to state that 'The question of whether the release of racial tension through humour is problematic has received little attention.'

Humour can often be ambiguous and deliberately prone to a range of readings. This ambiguity reflects what has been described as its polysemic nature, as irony, context and a plethora of meanings are spelled out with Weaver's (2010) use of a 'rhetorical triangle'. Weaver (2011) draws on ideas originating from Aristotle and developed in critical discourse analysis by Richardson (2006) of the arguer (teller), audience (receivers) and argument (story). In addition, it is commonly stated in humour studies that there are three theories of humour – Incongruity, Superiority and Relief (Critchley 2002; Weaver 2011; Ostrower 2015). I draw on each theme opportunistically in this chapter as there is such a complementary overlap across them. The idea of *superiority* can be seen where some of the stories of racism in this chapter resonate with ideas of humour that argue the perpetrators of racist acts are subverted and notions of superiority over them displace feelings of anger, ambivalence or hurt. Clarke (1998) explains that humour can cause two people to laugh for apparently different reasons. He states that receivers can sometimes laugh because of the sense of superiority ensuing from the teller while the teller may laugh because of the repressed emotion and tension that alleviates the psychic stress of such experiences. Superiority and relief can be initially viewed as functions of humour, whereas incongruity suggests more about the form humour takes.

Theories of *relief* often draw from Freud's (1991 [1960]) work on feelings of release: that is, if anxiety were not dispatched this way it would cause some psychic harm to the victims of racism. Weaver (2011) argues that it was Aristotle who first made the links between humour and *incongruity*, yet many argue that it is incongruity that significantly contributes to the structure or techniques used in the sharing of stories to evoke situations. Some of these situations can be nonsensical with a view to subverting an event to emphasise humour and therefore the teller's preferred reading of a story (Critchley 2002). Weaver (2011) explored incongruity in relation to how racialised groups reversed racist words to take away their power by delivering a reverse semantic effect. For incongruity to work there must be a juxtaposition of two or more objects that lack consistency, harmony, propriety or conformity (Berger 1998, cited in Weaver 2011: 18). Critchley (2002: 4) goes on to affirm this in relation to jokes:

> In order for the incongruity of the joke to be seen as such, there has to be congruence between joke structure and social structure – no social congruity, no comic incongruity.

Weaver (2010) uses the term 'resistance humour' to describe a discourse positioned in opposition to the perceived racism perpetrated by others, yet this is only partially my aim. Though I am concerned with how humour is used to ameliorate experiences of racism I am not solely concerned with the specific use of racist jokes or banter as starting points for rhetorical subversion. The aim of this chapter is more broad and encompassing. This chapter is concerned with the everyday strategic use of humour techniques in storytelling, given that the recourse to humour presents an opportunity to see it working in a way that is less trivial in nature for those affected by racism in sport (Clarke 1998).

Methodology

This chapter explores the rhetorical dynamics of humour in storytelling with Black football coaches in England as they share experiences of everyday racism. Delgado and Stefancic (2001: 39) describe the storytelling of Black and minoritised ethnic groups as a way to 'open a window onto ignored or alternative realities'. Where dominant groups have little understanding of how minority groups experience their sport then storytelling can help to facilitate understanding by 'bridging the gap'. In this chapter the techniques used to share stories of racism become the focus for the analysis of the role of humour.

Stories can reveal a different everyday reality to the one that is 'known', thus revealing 'unknowns' for a new critical consideration of issues. Stories can also give voice, or as hooks (1989) might suggest, 'teach to transgress' and make visible those who have historically been marginalised. In relation to notions of humour as resistive the Black coaches' focus group offers a chance to explore Delgado and Stefancic's idea of 'counter-storytelling'. Counter-storytelling is sometimes used to illustrate the destructive function of dominant discourses by offering an alternative reading. For example, in one of the few studies of humour in sport, Robidoux (2012) used storytelling in his research with First Nation hockey players to demonstrate how their humour can be used to better understand their racialised context. He used illustrated humour as a technique of empowerment and relief of racial tension.

As Delgado and Stefancic (1999; 2001) suggest, stories should be able to name and challenge forms of oppression and prejudice. Therefore, stories should also be capable of contributing to their dismantling. Bowers (2005) describes the power that can accrue through storytelling, and the storytelling process often afforded to those who may have been in less fortunate social positions. Through using elements of humour it can be seen how Black coaches reimagine protagonists and everyday forms of oppression in sport as part of their storytelling. It can enable a demystification and disruption of oppressive forces while enhancing the wellbeing of those that have suffered from such processes.

Methods and analysis

In this study, nine Black and minoritised ethnic coaches were included in a pilot focus group to facilitate the sharing of experiences of racism in sport. Each of the coaches self-identified as Black and were part of a network for established, qualified and experienced Black football coaches in England. Access was facilitated through a coordinator and each coach voluntarily consented to contributing to the study. Focus groups have been very successful in putting a group of acquaintances at ease and enabling subject matter, guided by the researcher, to develop ideas that even the researcher may not have initially anticipated (Gunaratnam 2003; Gratton and Jones 2004). Participants who are known to each other are more likely to feel relaxed, especially where the subject matter can be sensitive. The focus group was made up of predominantly African Caribbean men (7) and South Asian (2: 1M/1F) coaches.

The coaches were introduced to the aims of the focus group to share and explore experiences of racism in football. Humour was not divulged as an objective of the study to ensure that the group was not led toward attempting humorous or comedic anecdotes. This approach enabled any techniques of humour within the storytelling to emerge naturally. Pseudonyms are used throughout. In addition, the focus group was digitally captured with a camcorder and a boundary microphone voice recorder. Perakyla (2005: 510) suggests that where data is more 'naturally occurring' as in focus groups there is a chance that the way the interaction is recorded may ignore or marginalise key pieces of data. It is recognised that in the telling of stories, the sharing of instructive and sometimes ambiguous tales, the text does not necessarily share the body language and non-verbal cues that occur in social settings. In addition to a field diary, this multi-modal approach favoured by ethnographers offers a richer and deeper quality of data that will enable a more sophisticated examination of the interactions in the focus groups.

Critical race scholars have been conscious of the contradictions between action and behaviour and the need to represent what is happening from the point of view of racialised actors (Duster, Twine Warren et al. 1999). This has led to research embracing social justice and transformation that challenge established ideologies in sport (Carrington 2010; Hylton 2012). Privileging the Black voice through a plethora of techniques has become popular in CRT research, especially storytelling and counter-storytelling methods as ways to 'hear and understand the voices' that are rarely heard (Bell 1992). This chapter presents rich description in an extended theoretical account to get at what Charmaz argues goes beyond the overt to the 'tacit, liminal, and the implicit' (2005: 513). A grounded theory approach more closely aligned to the work of Charmaz was used to allow the major themes from the telling of stories to emerge. Perakyla (2005) describes a grounded theory approach as a set of guidelines that lead researchers to build mid-range theories through systematic data analysis and the reworking of possible readings of data and development of key concepts.

To aid this process of analysis I draw on use of the 'rhetorical triangle' that considers the significance and influence of the arguer (teller), audience (receivers) and argument (story) (Weaver 2011: 5). This enables a more convenient examination of the context of the storyteller, the audience, and the content and rhetorical structure of the argument. The arguer, the audience and the argument is the dynamic structure within which the 'humorous' is explored. In addition, Berger's

(2013) typology of forty-five techniques of humour enabled an ordering of approaches to storytelling that revealed an alternative perspective on the content of the stories shared (see Table 6.1). Other factors influencing the reading of each story included non-verbal communication and style of delivery.[1] The place of humour within this telling is where we now turn.

Findings

These findings reflect themes emerging from the coaches' focus group. They include stories of betrayal, White privilege, violence and multiple forms of racism. The group spoke across a large oval table in a room where they regularly met and therefore were comfortable in the setting and in each other's company. It is also imperative to note that some of the stories were *humourless* in the context of Berger's (2013) typology, Weaver's use of the rhetorical triangle (2010a; 2011a) and the three major themes of relief, superiority and incongruity found in the humour studies literature. In this context stories were chosen based on their potential to enable an examination of these signifiers of humour in a natural social environment. However, the first story shared by Kurt did not use humour. Kurt's 'matter of fact' telling of his experience was indicative of a number of the conversations in the focus group as highlighted by Gary who stated that:

> But I think when you tell stories, *your life* is a story of fighting against racism, so to pick out a story is difficult, it just seems like a conveyor belt of a process, day-by-day, moment-by-moment. And you try to think about 'how do I stay in my story and keep my sanity about who I am actually as a black person?'
>
> *(Emphasis added)*

It was neither easy nor straightforward for members of the group to pick experiences to share. Many of the experiences were purely statement of fact and delivered without any discernible tropes of humour. However, Gary reflected on broader issues in relation to the Black experience in the UK when he stated that it was difficult to choose one example from a plethora of others. In some ways, the mundanity of some of his everyday experiences did not seem to him to add up to a 'big' or interesting story. Awareness of microaggressions inevitably requires a critically informed 'race' consciousness, thus making them highly slippery and difficult to articulate. Nevertheless, all of the stories were useful and how they were shared was instructive.

Kurt was the first to break the ice and speak, and was choosing his words so as not to name names or implicate anyone in the football establishment. He told the group about how he felt he had been racially discriminated against in a high-level coaching assessment. He was unsure if it was due to his Jamaican accent or his Black skin though he knew there was a problem because the White coaches ignored him when it was his turn to do his coaching assessment. Kurt felt that no one wanted to take part in his session. With some emotion and indignation he went on to say:

And when it was my time to do my session, no-one – no-one was willing to participate, and the assessor said to them 'You must participate in all of the session' … and you tell me say no one participate in mine?! Not one person participate [sic]. And, to tell you the truth, I was going to say something and I looked at myself, and I said 'What does it matter?'

Kurt's use of the turn 'what does it matter?' suggests more than ambivalence or resignation on his part. It hints at the everyday weariness of negotiating subtle and ambiguous racism that cause people like him to calculate the potential for success were they to challenge such behaviours. 'What does it matter?' in the context of these coaches seemed to resonate with them as their non-verbal communication through body language and the occasional nod signified acceptance, more than disbelief, that racial discrimination occurs in this way in football. In a more diverse group there might have been some scepticism about the meanings of the White coaches' behaviour, whether Kurt had misinterpreted the situation, or perhaps that it was a one-off scenario. Yet there was no question in this focus group, from any of the coaches for clarification or qualification, which would suggest that Kurt's story is one that reveals part of the lived reality for these Black coaches.

In following Kurt's sharing, Bucky (Asian male) started with an example of what Freud (1991 [1960]) would describe as relief (or release) through humour. This took some tension out of the atmosphere and offered some indication of how humour is used as a form of resistance. Following Kurt's serious claims of racism Bucky stated:

I can call this little section 'name, shame and blame' if I really wanted to. I won't name them, but I'll certainly shame them and I'll definitely blame them!

Bucky began brightly with what Berger (2013) would describe as wordplay and a tone that gave the impression that he was about to tell an intriguing story. He outlined a situation at a UEFA B^2 coaching course where the coach leading the sessions over the whole fortnight chose to call him 'Gunga Din' in reference to the colonised and exploited Indian character in Rudyard Kipling's poem of British rule in India. The use of the term Gunga Din in this context emphasises the coach assessor's confidence that the use of racial epithets in the company of other pre-dominantly White coaches was acceptable. Maybe the White players were afraid to challenge the authority of the coach educator and unwittingly reinforced Kurt's experiences of racism in football? Kurt's experience also resonates with King's (2004) research into 'race' and football that highlights the expectation that Black coaches relegate their own identities to fit into a privileged culture of whiteness. He offers more on this story and draws on some tropes of Weaver's (2010) rhetorical triangle in the story (argument), the way he told the story (arguer) and the coaches' reception of it (audience) to make his point:

This was 1996, and he kept on going 'Oh, Gunga Din, can you do this, Gunga Din, can you do that.'! Well, the way I saw it, OK, is that I wanted to get the award. I didn't feel at that point in time ... Everyone else found that, you know, it was slightly humorous, everyone had a little laugh about it, OK. But it's like anything ... I felt that at that point in time there were two ways I could have dealt with it. I could have not turned up and not finished the course. I could have carried on, got the award, and dealt with it afterwards. But I was slightly naïve, even then, to be honest with you.

Unlike a traditional joke, the use of humour in the sharing of stories of racism does not necessitate laughter or spontaneous applause. Bucky's story was not only a descriptive sharing of a racist experience that was recognised as such in the focus group, but it also repositioned him within the story because he took the moral high ground in not reacting to the blatant racism of the coach assessor or the 'banter' in the group.

Bucky's re-envisioned superiority to the racist coach enabled him to share how racism can not only manifest itself but demonstrate how others condone and reinforce it through acquiescence. While doing this he also offered an argument for when to navigate and resist racism in football. On balance, he did not see a benefit to openly resisting the coach educator or the group racism, as it would have affected his future income. Yet it is clear for many in their research into racism and whiteness in football, such as Jones (2002) and King (2004), that 'getting on' comes with a price. The price of not challenging such engrained racism is that it maintains the hierarchies and boundaries between ingroups and outgroups, stereotypes and racialised differentiation. Further, the antiracist potential to 'rob commonsense racism of its power' is also lost in those moments (Hynes and Scott 2015).

Bucky's story about football coach education, partially enabled by tropes of humour, is brought to the meeting room and shared in the way Yosso (2005) would describe as cultural wealth, a type of under-researched form of cultural capital. It is likely to have assisted others in the room to make future decisions that would help them, through an increase in what Yosso would term 'navigational' capital, to manage football coaching culture more pragmatically (Yosso 2005). Consequently, with all of the caveats of acting versus not acting, the coaches may also have an improved understanding of how to use their 'resistance' capital more strategically: when do I push back, and under what circumstances?

At this point in the chapter it would be no surprise for readers to expect more traditional signs of humour in these stories. Hence it is worthwhile reiterating that none of the stories incorporated joke telling, and that most of the stories required a theoretically informed reading. There were a number of stories about experiencing racism, though not all drew on tropes of humour. Bucky's story followed Kurt's and yet the next one, Lanky's, drew on more obvious tropes of incongruity, superiority, absurdity and even a comic chase (see Table 6.1). He began his story by setting out a scene where he was playing at a high level. As an ex-professional player he talked about a game where a spectator ran onto the pitch:

TABLE 6.1 Techniques of humour according to category

Language	Allusion, Bombast, Definition, Exaggeration, Facetiousness, Insults, Infantilism, Irony, Misunderstanding, Over literalness, Puns/wordplay, Repartee, Ridicule, Sarcasm, Satire
Logic	Absurdity, Accident, Analogy, Catalogue, Coincidence, Comparison, Disappointment, Ignorance, Mistakes, Repetition, Reversal, Rigidity, Theme and Variation, Unmasking
Identity	Before/after, Burlesque, Caricature, Eccentricity, Embarrassment, Exposure, Grotesque, Imitation, Impersonation, Mimicry, Parody, Scale, Stereotype
Action	Chase, Slapstick, Speed

Source: Adapted from Berger (2013: 47).

> I was playing for Axxx City against Bxxx United at [stadium], and we were winning the game … And you know as with most games, five minutes to go, knackered, away from home, decide to go down, bad ankle, you know, just to get a breather, just to slow it down, do you know what I mean? Waste time. And everyone knows what you're doing. But then obviously getting up … as the physio was dealing with me … out of the corner of my eye … see a fan running onto the pitch … shouting 'you black bastard!, you black bastard!, you black bastard!' So I'm kind of like … 'OK, what do I do now!?'

Lanky's turn to two of Berger's (2013) comic tropes of absurdity and a chase scene masked the grievousness of this emotionally hurtful and potentially dangerous and violent experience; not least because he was caught out while feigning injury, which offered a more obvious comic twist. It also acts as another example of the burden of abuse that Black players have to endure relative to their White counterparts (see Holland 1997). This coupled with Lanky's distinctive, cheeky regional twang meant that his sociable, almost staccato delivery distracted the audience from the more heinous elements of his story – he was attacked by a racist. After describing how the fan was intercepted Lanky reflected upon other professional Black players' experiences of abuse and the need for him to do his utmost to resist such occurrences. In beginning with that initial comic release of tension he finished with a sharp political point that emphasised the theme of superiority:

> 'Do I report it or do I just let it go?' … So I just said to myself – and remembering that the guys before me and what they'd had to go through, 'I can't not do this.' And it was kind of the loneliest journey, you know, going to court by myself, going up to Bxxx by myself to give evidence … The guy sent me this letter apologising to the staff and all that kind of stuff … as they do. But in my brain I was going 'No … I have to make a stand here!'

Turning back to Bucky: he recounted how after achieving success in the racially charged UEFA B award he encountered another type of racism that reflected the broader social stereotyping of South Asian men, while at the same time reinforcing the myths of racial stereotypes in football. Bucky's second example is replete with Berger's use of humour techniques that include absurdity, before/after, disappointment, embarrassment, exposure, ignorance and sarcasm. His experience of racism proceeded thus:

> I got the UEFA B, and he [the coach educator] also said 'Within a year you can maybe go for [the] A Licence.' So then I left it a couple of years and then in [year] I got the sponsorship to go for the A License, and the open prison that is Lilleshall[3] was beckoning. I suppose … driving up there, I was told it was a 9.30 start. I left my house, I felt, in plenty of time. But there weren't really many satnavs at that time […] so I was kind of running late. And I kind of got there … Once I got into Lilleshall I couldn't find the car parking. I got a car parking space, probably about five minutes late. Rushed out. Ran down to reception. I had all my paperwork with me. Got to reception, said to the lady 'I'm Bucky Fizzan, I'm doing the A Licence.' [The receptionist said] 'Yeah, it's the introductions, second floor.' Strolled up to the second floor, knocked on the door – 'Coach Educator'. Opened the door. And the first thing he said to me was 'No one called a taxi here, mate, you're in the wrong place!' And I brought out my papers and said 'I'm here for the A Licence, my name's Bucky Fizzan.' And he went 'Oh, sorry, sorry … misunderstanding.'

The audience reception was impassive and taciturn in response. There was a collective edginess across the room as Bucky spoke, accompanied by the occasional nod of recognition, visible shock or shake of the head at key moments of the story. The coaches were respectful and seemingly disgusted but their demeanour was one of awareness and acceptance, if not accepting, of football culture. A football culture that in their research on the experiences of elite level football coaches Bradbury, van Sterkenburg et al. (2015) state is continually experienced through stereotyping and notions of unsuitability.

Simon was the next coach to present the group with a story, though this one was closest to a traditional comic anecdote. Yet, once the comic markers are removed that make the story more palatable and less traumatic for him to share, and the group to hear; it reveals a horrific personal story that would leave most feeling hurt and vulnerable. Simon was a big, confident charismatic man who launched into the telling of this story as though he had shared it a few times. However, Simon had not told his children this story, which says something about the severity of the content. He uses humour techniques that draw on earlier theories of incongruence, while Berger's (2013) humour techniques are heavily represented by the use of absurdity, before/after, bombast, burlesque, disappointment, exposure, ignorance, impersonation, insults, irony, mimicry, wordplay, ridicule and unmasking, that coalesce into this one story of betrayal, racism and ultimately superiority:

I'll have a go. I'm Simon Fairweather. Despite my youthful good looks I'm actually [age] … And I was happy to support – don't know really why, but I had to support a team called Axxxxx United. I went to watch them in the '80s, and they were the most vehemently racist group of supporters you've ever heard … This is the story that I'm telling this group. I haven't told this to my kids. But I remember going to watch Axxxxx play Wolves away in the Cup. We lost one-nil. Before the game, there was loads of bother, and there were loads of Wolverhampton lads – black, white and indifferent – chasing Axxxxx supporters, because Axxxxx had a big National Front there. I went with this lad – and this lad now … I can name him, he's actually a [job/ location]. And he was a good guy, a mate of mine, I'd known him for not that long, but I'd known him for a while. And I was 17, 18. Twenty minutes into the game, we're in the away end, the Axxxxx supporters, and the whole away end started singing 'We hate niggers' and as I looked to my right, they're all singing it – I looked to my left… but the guy I was with was singing 'We hate niggers.' The bit I remember was the veins coming out of his neck…he was singing it with such venom! […] Two hours later, he was at Wolverhampton train station, shitting himself and holding on to my arm because I was the nigger that was going to keep him alive… the reason I tell the story about Axxxxx is because two hours, he hated niggers and at Wolverhampton train station, 'Protect me Simon, you're a big black guy, they won't hit you!'

Here Simon shares an anecdote that emphasises the banality of bigotry, and the ambivalent ignorance of a 'friend' who in a matter of hours openly shared what Hughey (2011) and Picca and Feagin (2007) describe as the backstage talk of White people. Simon's friend was able to enjoy the security of whiteness in the hostile football arena while thoughtlessly subjugating *his friend* in what one might perceive he would see as harmless banter. Muller, van Zoonen et al. (2007) argue that when soccer fans who are not labelled as racists commit racist acts they often deny accountability. As a result, the burden of claiming that racism took place fell on Simon. Simon's 'friend' later showed a more vulnerable front-stage away supporter identity that emphasised the contingent nature of embodied identities when he pleaded for help from the racialised body that he earlier denigrated. Sullivan and Tuana (2007: 1) would describe this behaviour as an ignorance of injustice and an 'obliviousness to racism and white domination'.

Following on from Simon's bizarre experience the group discussed notions of hegemonies (if not in those terms), internalised racism and collusion in Black communities, in addition to issues of racialised and gendered identities. Yet during all of this, an example of humour as relief emerged as we approached the end of this, sometimes tense, group conversation. As Bob reflected on his position as an equalities tutor, an exchange ensued that not only drew on a number of Berger's humour techniques, but also engaged notions of exaggeration, ridicule, stereotypes/ irony and facetiousness.

At this point, Bob was about to share his experience of equalities tutors in football, whom he argued 'struggled to keep their racism shackled'. He went on to make statements like, it is really frightening to 'hear quite overt racists kind of contorting themselves to take on the new language'. And how during the training 'I was still getting racist remarks from other equality tutors …' And yet before completing the preamble to his story Bob engaged in what could be described as the most obvious light-hearted, good-humoured exchange. This exchange with a number of the coaches enabled a sense of release for the group through the pressure valve of laughter. It was a distraction from the serious nature of the topic that reinforced the cohesion of the group through a flurry of dialogue that lifted the atmosphere to enable a challenging reality to be shared:

BUCKY: I think you did me as well, Bob [Assessed him as a tutor].

BOB: Oh, I done your assessment? Yeah.

BUCKY: You failed me!

[Laughter and comments]

BOB: Do you know what? I'm going to put my hand up to that one. Bucky was totally crap.

[Laughter]

BOB: I only passed him …

SURIA (SOUTH ASIAN, FEMALE, INTERRUPTING): Because he's Asian?!

[Laughs]

BOB: We colluded together. That's obviously what we will do when we get into positions of control …!

[Laughter]

This was the point in the discussion where there were more obvious concerted attempts at recognisable humour than at any other time in over an hour's focus group. It is reasonable to suggest at this point in proceedings that relief from the whole process was being experienced across the group. This exchange was at a point in the discussion when the group had relaxed in each other's company and after some anxiety had built up to this opportunity for more traditional joking in-between the storytelling. Yet these quips were clearly drawing on good natured sarcasm, while the satire in the exchange with Suria alluded to White backlash notions of the Black creep into the upper echelons of sporting organisations while the allusion is established using techniques of incongruence; facetiousness and stereotype.

Conclusion

With an application of Berger's typology, the rhetorical triangle and humour studies themes of Incongruity, Superiority and Relief, a nuanced understanding of the rhetorical dynamics of this focus group emerges (Berger 1995; Weaver 2010; 2011; 2013). Depending on the context, for these Black coaches techniques of humour may indeed entail a relief from tension, psychic harm and a strengthening of a group – equally it may signify a resistance to suffering. Reid (2015: 231) describes humour here as giving serious issues voice and status. hooks' (cited in McNair 2008: 204) description of language as action, as resistance and struggle is illustrated as humour enables some often taboo subjects to be raised. The coaches' stories were not systematically infused with everyday humour though the strategic use of these techniques hinted at a celebration of survival in the face of adversity (Bowers 2005).

A reading of the coaches' narratives emphasises Ostrower's (2015) observation that humour emerges when we experience negative emotion. In this respect it is argued that humour can be used as a device for 'serious purposes', it can also heal and hurt as we saw in Kurt's opening story and Bucky's distressing 'Gunga Din' experience (Mulkay 1988). We also saw evidence that 'stories told by underdogs are frequently ironic or satiric', one of these purposes is for 'out-group realities to circulate as a counter reality' (Delgado, 2000: 60–61). It can be argued that the coaches' stories assisted each other to become more conscious of how to navigate a racialised sport. In some cases these strategies were implemented for survival, for fear of being cast as antisocial, 'humourless', or even unemployable. These lived experiences are recounted in a rhetorical triangle that repositions the teller in what have been humiliating, traumatic and disempowering situations. Perpetrators are also repositioned as the teller is empowered for the benefit of self and the audience. Inferiority, subordination and feelings of oppression are turned into superiority, and everyday social arrangements are made incongruous, and racialised difficulties are at least partially ameliorated as strategies to deal with future microaggressions are shared.

In regard to many of the stories, once the signs of humour are taken away, they reveal microaggressions recognisable as insults, invalidations and assaults (Burdsey 2011). For example, Bucky's taxi driver and Gunga Din incidents; Simon's debilitating National Front story; Lanky, Kurt and Bob's experiences that without tropes of humour would heighten the audience and the teller's anxieties, feelings of marginalisation and oppression.

The use of humour as defence against the multiple effects of racism has the potential to empower the Black coaches' voices, transform their felt experiences and how they see themselves and others, and engage them in sharing cultural wealth. The polysemic nature of the coaches' stories also enables them to retain a double meaning requiring of interpretation as serious content is maintained regardless of the level of the delivery or tropes of humour within. This chapter reveals a significant need for further explorations into humour studies as a tool to understand how racism is resisted by Black and minoritised ethnic groups in sport. The import of such a research agenda for the future direction of humour studies in sport should be clear as we touch upon the subtleties of humour (Watson 2015). It appears that humour is neither 'trivial' nor 'playful' in the negative sense, and that we cannot ignore how it has been used here in a plethora of ways to act as resistance to racism in sport.

Notes

1 In some cases the use of patois infused some of the conversations and required interpretation.
2 The UEFA B Licence is the third highest level coaching award in European football. Second is the UEFA A Licence, followed by the final Pro Licence.
3 Lilleshall is a Sport England national sports centre.

7

CRITICAL RACE THEORY MATTERS IN SPORT

> It seems fair to say that most critical race theorists are committed to a programme of scholarly resistance, and most hope that scholarly resistance will lay the groundwork for wider-scale resistance.
>
> *(Bell 1995: 900)*

W. E. B. Du Bois' claim about the ongoing significance of the colour line is reiterated here by Derrick Bell (above) who advocated that such ideas are still relevant today. Bell also argued that critical race theorists are recognisable by their concern with the place of 'race' and racism in society that centres them, while specific intersecting challenges span disciplines that make for a diverse range of interests. A focus on sport here has reaffirmed its place as a significant socio-cultural arena where social mores, norms and ideologies can be created, perpetuated and resisted. With *'race' as the point of departure for critique, not the end of it* (Leonardo 2005: xi) the context of sport remains contested and complex. Like other areas of social concern sport forces activist scholars to *struggle where they are* (Gillborn 2016). 'Race' matters in sport and critical 'race' scholars recognise the dangers of 'race' neutrality and politics that leave racialised terrain undisturbed (Burdsey 2011; Carrington 2013; Coram and Hallinan 2017; Hawkins, Carter-Francique et al. 2017). Though this approach can be the path of least resistance for some such a strategy remains the gift of those who will gain privilege from it, or those less 'race' conscious (Sue 2003; Picca and Feagin 2007).

Many will view sport as unimportant without thought for how it surreptitiously reinforces positions on 'race' and dispositions to racism. For example, Serena Williams' perception of how she is viewed in regards to Maria Sharapova signals how stereotypes, gendered racism and class dynamics work to reproduce views of her that become shorthand for other women and men in tennis and beyond (Guardian Sport 2017). Williams' reading of how she is read by others as looking 'mean' because she is Black hints at the prevalence of racial bias and assumptions that find their way into sport and from there into other social arenas. The racial mechanics that lead to shaping how Williams is viewed as an elite tennis player give some indication of how stereotypes and assumptions lead to other behaviours on the sidelines, in the classroom, and the boardroom. The under-theorised nature of 'race' and sport, racism online and offline, the prevalence of whiteness, privilege and supremacy, and the paucity of Black leaders within reinforces the view that the meritocracy of sport remains aspirational. While 'race' remains the miner's canary for the more insidious, odious tensions in sport and society, Critical Race Theory endorses a critical engagement with shaming colour lines and contesting racial dynamics in sport and society (Guinier and Torres 2003).

This book examines the place of 'race' and its intersections, and racism on topics in sport that many would overlook. Historically these issues have been marginalised, under-researched and under-theorised. Regardless of the topic, a CRT critique in sport, on for example, ice skating, tennis, swimming, governance, college sports, humour, gendered racism, basketball, whiteness, motor racing, the seaside or even cycling can take ordinary phenomena and make them extraordinary; revealing how everyday realities from the living room to the boardroom are replete with signatures of injustice and the potential for resistance and change. As structural racisms and patriarchy tessellate with intersecting identities, microaggressions, aversive and unconscious/implicit bias, at institutional and micro levels, whiteness and White supremacy do the everyday work of maintaining 'race' talk, power relations and the status quo.

Colourblindness and meritocracy facilitate discourses of inclusion in sport that are persuasive and attractive to many while making the targets of antiracism and anti-oppression slippery and elusive. It is not a matter of common acceptance that structural practices of racism embedded elsewhere are likely to be present in the sport that we watch, participate or work in. To challenge ideas of the *sport for all* hyperbole it becomes a challenge first to establish the racialised processes and outcomes tied into philosophies of meritocracy and practices in sport. For example, the critique of equal opportunities in local government sport policy implementation, in Chapter 1, required much more than evidence of racial disparities in the diversity of senior staff in local authorities that could be evidenced in human resources audits, but a more nuanced and critical examination of the way policy gaps emerged through institutionalised practices and micro-level behaviours. The symbiosis of institutional structures and agency are not immediately revealed to the professional gaze, yet the red flags appear where sustained racial disparities, racism and discrimination can be revealed and explained.

The red flags in this book appear in different ways, requiring of us attention in how we consider the coaching landscape and the place of 'race' and gender in coaching and leadership. Puwar (2004: 33) argues that the universal individual in many bureaucracies and professions does not include everyone because the symbolism of White maleness becomes *the indicator* of the prototype of a leader; the natural occupant of higher positions.

Thus different bodies belonging to 'other' places are in one sense out of place as they are 'space invaders'.

It is generally understood that there are disparities in sport and society, though there is a lack of clarity among key stakeholders about how these gaps can be reduced (Amara and Henry 2010; Walseth 2016; Long, Fletcher et al. 2017). Similarly, the effort to improve the diversity of leadership in sport and any subsequent successes should not engender complacency, especially when we do not know what these contexts will reveal for new incumbents (Regan and Feagin 2017). Alternatively, what does improved diversity mean for the traditional occupants of sporting hierarchies and what can we learn from their circumstances? Do we simply 'count heads' (Puwar 2004) to suggest that 'race' no longer matters or do we continue to ask questions about the preponderances of specific masculinities, institutional cultures and unremarked whiteness?

We should be aware of notions of resistance to racism in sport though we are not fully conversant with the forms that resistance might take (Testa and Amara 2016; Hawkins, Carter-Francique et al. 2017). The use of humour cited in Chapter 6 illustrated how it can be used as a device to channel forms of resistance through cultural wealth while sharing techniques to navigate oppressive systems. Humour, rather than joke telling, was much more subtle and foundational to individual and group wellbeing. Its ready and intuitive use was also reflective of the regularity of its application to long-term and everyday circumstances. Drawing on such techniques offers a different discourse for moments that disempower or need 'retelling' as a counter narrative. Resistance for survival in an everyday sense eases the psyche and the systemic racialised injustices that social commentators over the years have aimed to disrupt in theory and practice (Carrington 2012; Fitzpatrick and Santamaría 2015; Coram and Hallinan 2017).

In discussions on the political investment in conducting research on 'race' and racism, Rollock (2013) explains the tensions and power relations that scholars experience in managing the research process. Working with and against racialised power relations and the (dis)empowering privileges of whiteness is an everyday challenge for critical researchers. Rollock (2013) referred to how Black scholars were 'speaking back' from the margins in the way that the White researchers in Chapter 3 were 'speaking from the centre'. Antiracist and social justice agendas do not begin from a standing start, and whether speaking back or speaking from the centre these struggles and travails take on a different slant. 'Race', gender, class and other intersections affect researcher identities, agendas and politics in a way that is only partially documented in this book and by authors like Rollock (2013), Duster, Twine Warren et al. (1999), Hylton (2012), Tuhiwai Smith (2012), Mowatt, French et al. (2013) and Roberts (2013).

'Speaking from the centre' has the potential to reinforce the marginality of those traditionally absent from the academy, while privileging established histories and epistemologies. Yet the dangers of not speaking from positions of strength or privilege is to dysconsciously ignore how one is implicated in maintaining racial hierarchies and the status quo. Though in the words of Razack (1999: 37),

There are landmines strewn across the path wherever storytelling is used [...] it should never be used uncritically [...] its potential as a tool for social change is remarkable, provided we pay attention to the interpretive structures that underpin how we hear and how we take up the stories of oppressed groups.

The device of storytelling is used in a number of the chapters as a way to privilege voices and stories worthy of more attention and understanding. In each case space was enabled to facilitate a challenge to ideologies of domination and power that revealed alternative ways to approach research. Analogous to the way that Lawrence and Tatum (2004) were intrigued to comprehend whether White teachers' racial identities influenced their practice, it was thought provoking to reveal researchers in Chapter 3 explaining how their White privilege and identities did a similar thing. The White researchers' privilege was used to frame their self-articulated critical consciousness necessary for important scholarship on 'race'. The act of eschewing White 'raceless-ness' had a direct impact on the research process and stores of knowledge used to underpin such work (Blaisdell 2009; Trepagnier 2010; Gillborn 2011).

The researchers in Chapter 3 demonstrated that their whiteness necessarily brought them to a position where 'race' and racism were experientially less well understood than other aspects of their lives, yet significantly their politics enabled a recognition of a differently experienced racialised self. As Ladson-Billings and Tate IV (2006: 22–23) argue, the power of whiteness through its 'property functions' leads to circumstances that can privilege behaviours that conform to dominant norms and practices, social, cultural and economic privileges, and rights to include and exclude in a plethora of fashions. Where the influence of whiteness on practice has been recognised, the danger of racial disparities being sustained and racial critique misinformed has been disrupted (Lawrence and Tatum 2004).

Sport as a site of racial domination and resistance is further emphasised by how we experience it (Leung 2005). Where Whine (1997) cautions us that the internet is an arena with sufficient conditions for discrimination to thrive we saw it in Chapter 5 in the case of Tiger Woods and the social media campaign of the anti-racism sport organisation Kick it Out (Kick it Out 2016). Offline and online interactions shift traditional notions of embodiment. Physicality, while as much as it is constructed by 'race', becomes differently ambiguous and more challenging. Far from being 'race'-neutral, cyberspace is a site where we take our opinions, attitudes and ideologies and reproduce them. Though the dynamics of social interactions in a virtual environment are changed due to proximity, it is clear that sport online is little understood in regards to the operation of 'racial mechanics' (Kang 2003). Racial mechanics map others into racial categories that stimulate racial meaning and could be seen in operation in how online commentators in Chapter 5 conjured with Tiger Woods' racial background and the loaded meanings behind seemingly benign media headlines.

As Kick it Out (2016) has observed, internet platforms can be the problem or the solution, as they have attempted to operationalise limited resources to marshal resistance to hate speech and all forms of discrimination online. Hate speech is a vague concept that when defined can be countered in different countries by a plethora of different laws. In their mapping exercise on cyberhate, the Council of Europe (2012) recognised the challenge not only of defining hate speech but a need to recognise its peculiarities online. Hate speech was defined as,

> Covering all forms of expression which spread, incite, promote or justify racial hatred, xenophobia, anti-semitism, or other forms of hatred based on intolerance, including: intolerance expressed by aggressive nationalism, and ethnocentrism, discrimination and hostilities against minorities, migrants and people of immigrant origin.

The definition takes a wide-ranging view of hate speech and adopts a nonexhaustive approach to targeted groups. The Council of Europe also acknowledges that online 'cyberhate' requires an additional protocol to take into account the diversity of speech and sources from which hate can emerge online. The Council of Europe (2012: 9) added the following definition to the protocol to the Convention on Cybercrime to supplement its earlier broad definition:

> Additional Protocol to the Convention on Cybercrime. Article 2.1. For the purposes of this Protocol:
> 'racist and xenophobic material' means any written material and any image or any other representation of ideas or theories, which advocates, promotes or incites hatred, discrimination or violence, against any individual or group of individuals, based on race, colour, descent or national or ethnic origin, as well as religion if used as a pretext for any of these factors.

The same technologies being manipulated to subjugate can be the very resources used to disrupt racialised acts of denigration. However, because recourse to action differs across nations and continental regions, the global reach of online racists makes the task of combatting racism in sport online much more complex than in more traditional offline incidents. Where hate speech is challenged it is complicated by a need to maintain the democratic rights of individuals and groups' freedom of expression. Further it requires the skill set of specialists that can look beyond the words of a communication to understand what the impact might be of such sharing.

Far from being a frontier of social equality, the internet is a frontier of a different kind, more akin to a battleground: a contested frontier that requires multiple interventions and research to more fully comprehend the nature and extent of the problem for sport in virtual spaces. The danger with the internet is that it can be used almost like a 'smart' racist bomb that can be sent to its target without the perpetrators ever leaving their seats or having to face their victims. As a result, the pace of disturbing and damaging views about 'race' and its intersections, nation and xenophobia, can become a blur. Within this blur of online activity many people now feel more empowered to share hateful views, even offline, while putting into public office those who reflect such shocking views. This hints at the symbiosis of sport and society whether offline or online. While most people traditionally participate in sport offline, online domains have become popular and relatively censure-free spaces to share a whole range of views that pose a significant problem to understanding how racist ideologies are recreated and perpetuated with relative ease.

Cycling as a barometer of 'race' matters in sport

I wrote an article in *The Conversation* about how I experienced cycling as a Black man in the north of England (Hylton 2017a). It was provocatively entitled 'The Unbearable Whiteness of Cycling'. My main reason for writing this was to see if others had observed similar patterns that made 'race' salient in a sport that to my knowledge has not had a public conversation on the effects that 'race' and racial dynamics have had on how we enter, progress and experience the sport. Implicit within these observations was the desire to explore processes of inclusion and exclusion and the complexities related to intersections of 'race' with other identities, for instance gender and class (see also Hylton 2017b). The article was about how we understand the processes leading to the inclusion of differently raced bodies rather than anything more sinister.

The piece in *The Conversation* generated a lot of interest and readers were generous in sending links to organisations like Black Girls Do Bike (2017), which is an organisation that they say is about

> supporting a community of women of color who share a passion for cycling [...] We look to share positive images of ladies and their bikes to affirm the truth that black girls do indeed bike!

They (BGDB) do not state what led them to set up this organisation but I do hint at it in my *Conversation* article, and more specifically, promising racer Ayesha McGowan does emphasise that

> If I had seen another black person in cycling when I was a kid, maybe I would have been inspired to get into it sooner
>
> *(Edinburgh Festival of Cycling 2017)*

McGowan's tour of talks in the UK in the summer of 2017 focused on how she has 'climbed the gender and race ladder' and her journey to becoming 'the first female African-American professional cyclist'.

Like McGowan and the cyclists from Black Girls Do Bike, each July most cycling enthusiasts look forward to the start of the premier cycle race, the Tour de France. Where cycling is understood to have major economic and health benefits there are surprisingly few sources that explain the appeal, or otherwise, for the social groups that participate. Though the global market is valued at over 38 billion euros the constraints of the cycling environment for some social groups that might be seen as threats or opportunities are less well understood. For example, Steinbach, Green et al. (2011) report that gender, ethnicity and income affect cycling rates and preferences. In London, only one in three cyclists are women, and in a city where a third of the population identifies as Black, Asian and minority ethnic, 86 per cent of male cyclists and 94 per cent of female cyclists are White. To compound matters, the wealthier a person is in London the more likely they are to cycle. Depending on geography there are different participation histories for cycling. So, in London more men cycle than women yet in the Netherlands more women cycle than men (Green, Steinbach et al. 2010). Though there are regional and national differences that affect all of these variables, ethnicity, gender and socio-economics are significant factors. Cycling is a sport that has been described as globally very 'White' and limited in terms of which social groups participate (Seaton 2009). Cycling journalist Seaton (2009) explains that he could count most of the professional Black riders in the UK as there are so few. In addition, Olympic Team GB cycling coach David Brailsford told Seaton (2009) that,

> Breaking down the barriers to wider participation from black and ethnic minority groups remains the great unconquered goal for British cycling.

Despite the former mayor of London's strategy to increase cycling and the demographics of cycling in the capital there remains a firmly White, male and middle-class constituency of participants in the sport (Green, Steinbach et al. 2010). There is evidence of other reasons to cycle, or otherwise, that include fear of the road and other drivers, childcare, commuting, and security, yet little evidence of studies that consider ethnic differences. The literature review conducted for Transport for London by Green, Steinbach et al. (2010) identified ethnic segregation as an issue for some groups not wanting to cycle through 'White' areas in addition to the lack of infrastructure, cycle training, low levels of bike ownership and, significantly, *seeing people that looked like themselves* being a key facilitator across all population groups. Thus, many who identify as Black will not see the everyday normality of cycling that might enthuse their White counterparts. Doubts arise about identity and belonging where alienating imagery, the predominance of whiteness and closed social networks are in operation.

Where Steinbach, Green et al. (2011: 1124) ask the question *How do gendered, class and ethnic categories affect the uptake of cycling?* this section highlights the significance of how 'race' and racial processes in sport can affect attitudes to cycling in different contexts, at different levels of performance; and as reflective of structural and institutional racism. These instances challenge the mythology of sport as fair and equitable and reinforce it as a racially contested arena. It does this when micro-level (individual) experiences mesh with cultural and institutional racial bias and racism. As a series of connected incidents in a low-controversy sport (apart from blood doping), cycling is used here as an example of how *the familiar can be made strange* (Mills 1970).

As a keen cyclist I have reflected on the positive experiences of long rides in the company of friends. Over a number of years I have occasionally considered how the quality of my rides have differed depending on where I go and with whom. In one group I am hypervisible and in another I am invisible. I am hypervisible in a group of White friends, yet this is rarely made an issue by them or by others that see our peloton. The odd second look has never been followed by a remark though these uneasy, ambiguous and sometimes unwelcoming gazes can be interpreted in ways that could be viewed as microaggressive (Tate 2016). However, where I am invisible *my group is hypervisible* because they are all Black and are a real rarity in cycling circles. It is in this group where glimpses have turned into stares. It is in this group where passers-by have taken time to wind their windows down to hurl racial slurs in our direction. In and around Leeds in Yorkshire it does not take long to cycle out of the inner urban areas before entering the wonderful countryside, though in these 'White spaces' socio-cultural differences between those who inhabit these spaces and the cyclists become exaggerated and irritate those who implicitly police ingroup and outgroup relations.

These tensions are mirrored at loftier levels where the welcome for some world-class Black cyclists has been disturbing. The MTN-Qhubeka Tour de France team from Africa complained of racial abuse from other teams. The team was made up of a mix of Africans from Eritrea, Rwanda, South Africa and Algeria with US, Norwegian, Austrian and Australian riders. In what was described as a 'heat of the battle' exchange a victimised rider was issued with an apology while the offending cyclist's team expelled the rider in question and issued a statement of 'no tolerance for such behaviour' (Press Association 2015). Though the team has won tour events this incident is not isolated. The team principal, Douglas Ryder, added that in the previous year,

> One of the biggest teams in the world … in the Tour of Spain, when we were trying to bring one of our riders to the front going into the mountains, [said] *you guys don't belong here, fxxx off to the back of the bunch.*

According to Ryder, these talented Black riders have had to rely on the support of their White riding and management colleagues to gain acceptance, and even though Daniel Teklehaimanot has won the King of the Mountains polka dot jersey in the Tour de France, they have struggled to be accepted as cyclists because they are seemingly out of place in this 'White sport' (Press Association 2015). These incidents are in stark contrast to the ethos of the team name; Qhubeka means 'to progress' or 'to move forward'. Cycling is also a useful example to explain how racial processes and racism reinvent themselves across spaces, recreational and elite contexts. In the case of the US there is an added dimension that more clearly ties in a state-sponsored racial element to recreational cycling, to which we now turn.

In Chicago, cycling is observed to be racialised in a way that accentuates Critical Race Theory notions of the structurally embedded nature of racism. In a city where cycling patterns are overlaid with police citations the bulk of infractions occur in the least popular cycling spaces. Though statistics can only reveal part of a story, the disproportionality of these statistics raises serious concerns. These spaces are racialised as Black and the unequal share of the citations are issued to African Americans. Despite the popularity of cycling in predominantly White communities, over 8 years (2008–2016) the top ten citation areas include seven that are African American and three that are Latino (Wisniewski 2017). Police actions are seen as insensitive to the lack of cycling infrastructure for bike security and cycle paths, that forces some cyclists to use paths away from busy traffic. The issue is not purely about 'race', as class, diasporic movements and historical settlements form part of the larger story here. Real estate 'red lining' as practised by ex-NBA team owner Donald Sterling (see Hylton and Lawrence 2016) could also be factored into the reason why African American and Latino communities live in these spaces. These issues raise concerns over the victimisation of Black people in Chicago, and is reflected in other diverse areas in the US and internationally (Epp and Maynard-Moody 2014; Quinton 2015; Epp and Maynard-Moody 2016). In a mundane way infractions need police action, though in a more critical way they reveal racial processes at play that lead to the criminalisation of people because of how they look or cultural background when at leisure or on simple commutes to work (Glover 2009; Glynn 2014). Wisniewski (2017) states that,

> Some bike advocates and an elected official expressed concern that police may be unfairly targeting cyclists in black communities while going easier on law-breaking cyclists in white areas. Blacks, Latinos and whites each make up about a third of the city's residents, according to the U.S. Census Bureau.

Bloom (2017) is one of the few to establish a link between 'race' and bicycles when he discussed the use of bikes as part of a disproportionate aggressive policing strategy from the early 1970s in Washington DC. Bicycle stakeouts or stings have become a cutting edge to bicycle theft reduction policies in Washington. It was at a bicycle stakeout where African American Gregory Coleman was shot in 1972 for taking a bike he thought was his own stolen one. A policeman stated that the gun fell out of his holster and shot Coleman by accident (Bloom 2017). The racial pattern of the policing of city boundaries due to the enhanced mobility of ethnic populations is an aspect of cycling that he argues has been present since the late nineteenth century, though there is a paucity of research on this topic. Since the initial bike registration policy in Washington was repealed in 2008, there emerged the space for individual and institutional racial bias in the 'random inspections' that ensued. This registration policy underpinned the stop and search 'pre-textual stops' that led to the profiling and criminalisation of many Black communities. The profiling of suspicious behaviour or characters on the streets was subject to interpretation and therefore open to the racial profiling that has led to the over-citing and over-incarceration of Black people. In the 1970s the fear of bike gangs penetrating racialised city boundaries, co-constructed with the police an image of cycling requiring control, and yet when we explore the links between ethnicity and cycling we can see similar patterns of policing today.

These ruminations lead me to conclude that cycling is subject to the same social problems brought into other sports by wider dispositions to 'race' and racial bias (Duru 2011; Harrison 2013; Lorenz and Murray 2014). The familiar really is quite strange, though once we become aware of racial dynamics in cycling what should the key stakeholders in cycling do next? Indeed, what might begin to explain this state of affairs? Structural, institutional and individual racisms? In the US, the shift to the Right has been obvious, and for many seemingly unproblematic. The first term of the Republican Party in 2017 followed one of the most baffling and brutal presidential races in history where it seemed that misogyny, racism, xenophobia and ignorance were not only tolerated but led the strategy for a successful presidential campaign (Bhattacharya 2017). The confidence shown by many willing to bring their brand of 'alternative' politics to the fore reinforced the evidence of pernicious structural racism and patriarchy in the US as elsewhere. Analogous to this, the bike statistics between some of the areas differentiated by ethnicity, made it difficult to move beyond the problem of the Chicago police's institutionalised racism even when they are under surveillance from Black communities in Chicago (Bosman and Smith 2017). Over nine months in 2016 the low-income African American area of Austin received 321 citations compared to the five citations given to those in the well-off predominantly White area of Lincoln Park. It has been suggested that the bike stops are a pretext excuse for other searches, and in heavily policed areas where drug-related crime is a policy priority, biking fines are likely to be conflated with wider police strategies.

The Chicago police do not have a good record where 'race' is concerned. They have been consistently viewed as indiscriminately targeting and victimising Black people while their lack of accountability led them to accept that they were institutionally racist (Chicago Police Accountability Task Force Community Forum 2016). The mayor-appointed task force stated in its report that though the Chicago population is relatively evenly split between African Americans, White people and Latinos, the statistics reveal the disproportionate attention paid to Black communities.

> Black people were the subjects in 72 percent of the thousands of investigative street stops that did not lead to arrests during the summer of 2014.
>
> *(Davey and Smith 2016)*

In Chicago, there was also a culture of individual behaviour being ignored by commanders after excessive force was used. Imagine the difference in how some cyclists in Chicago experience their sport compared with others. Bosman and Smith (2017), reporting on the Chicago Task Force findings, outlined how an officer was found guilty of pointing a gun at teenagers on bikes suspected of trespassing. Sport is clearly a contested arena while everyday cyclists and even Tour de France competitors reveal that 'race' is significant in how others perceive them, associate with them and treat them. These incidents are not peculiar to Chicago.

New York City is also plagued with what has been described as 'the new stop and frisk' (Nwoye 2014). *Biking while Black* in New York City can lead to an infraction that leads to a prison sentence. The same disproportionate condemnation of racial profiling where *there are more sidewalk stops where there are more stop and frisks* where in 2009 and 2010 bike summonses were the third highest category of summons (Nwoye 2014). Cycling, like other sports is subject to the same social processes, and depending upon context and individual circumstances 'race' and racial processes present in ways that require a critical lens. Racial profiling is not limited to the police and can be the starting point for any number of interactions offline or online (Glover 2009; Foxton 2012).

The 'while Black' phenomenon

The stop and frisk bike stings (stop and search in the UK) pre-textual searches have been tagged with the tongue-in-cheek idea of 'while Black' that began with the experience of Black people being targeted for offences while driving (Harris 1997). 'Driving while Black' has now developed its own momentum where certain activities have the propensity to draw claims of racial profiling leading to disproportionate racial outcomes. The bicycle incidents would fall into this category, and 'cycling while Black' has been shown to be disproportionately problematic for Black people in comparison to their White counterparts. It demonstrates the inextricable complexities of 'race' in our lives and the inescapable trap of structural racism for the sport and leisure we participate in. For instance, consider booking a trip to a sporting event; this experience for some could make the difference between whether they travel again for such an event or give up a sport as a result of racism in the hospitality industry insinuating itself into a sport-related context. The racialised ignominies experienced through sport become indicative of broader social problems because racism is embedded in society. For example, the case of some people's experiences of Airbnb demonstrates how sporting contexts can be inextricably linked to other parts of our lives. Sport can affect or be affected in ways that may seem unconnected to significant parts of our social lives and may run parallel or contiguously through instances of microaggressions.

Racial bias: Airbnb

As identified in specific sporting examples in earlier chapters, similar controversy has shed light on the dangers of racial bias with the internet accommodation firm Airbnb. Airbnb has established a business model that allows homeowners to rent their properties to paying guests. It was found in a Harvard study (Luscombe 2014) that there was a pattern of White landlords rejecting requests from people with African American- or Latino-sounding names. Airbnb inadvertently opened its organisation up to bias and discrimination when it allowed its landlords and renters to reveal their identities. The Black guests also found their ability to get reservations was significantly improved when profile photos were changed for more neutral ones such as landscapes. Whether these behaviours were conscious or otherwise on the part of the landlords is immaterial given the racialised outcomes for those most affected. There was also an additional pattern of Black landlords charging less for the same properties rented by White landlords because they recognised the operation of racial prejudice in the marketplace. Airbnb's CEO stated,

> Airbnb has an obligation to be honest about our shortcomings, and do more to get our house in order. A part of the process has been learning how to fight explicit racism and implicit biases that can lead to discrimination.
>
> *(Weise 2016)*

This commitment from the Airbnb CEO led to its managers reacting to the flaws in its business model by establishing new procedures that included amending social identifiers, non-discrimination agreements, instant booking programmes, blocking landlords from booking places they have said were occupied, and also reworking its own hiring practices to challenge racial bias. The move to change its hiring practices reflects Airbnb's poor ethnic diversity and a desire to shift its organisational culture to reduce the chances of such errors occurring in the future. It has done this by establishing a 'Rooney Rule' policy that ensures that all senior staff recruitment pools include women and Black candidates (Staff 2016).

Conclusion

The relevance of critical race scholarship is as important today as it was in W. E. B. Du Bois' time. Just as any reading of society must consider the place of 'race' and racism, we must recognise that sport requires a critical lexicon that moves beyond the rhetoric of antiracism (Gillborn 2006). Applying a critical lens to sport necessitates an approach that acknowledges that racial power relations are at play and if left uncontested will remain to thrive. Racial processes in sport are often unspectacular and seemingly harmless, though their accumulated effects can be the difference between employment or unemployment, being scouted or cut, taking up one sport or another, or governing bodies achieving excellence or falling short.

Ways forward include increasing diversity in sport at a number of levels, such as improving the number of Black women leaders and academics. Their shared experiences of leading through the coaching and governance pathways bring a diversity of ideas to knowledge formation and policy communities. There are a number of examples where Black women and leadership has been incorporated into studies that extend our knowledge of 'race' and leadership (Sanchez-Hucles and Davis 2010; White 2010; Curtis 2014). Working with indigenous Australian women leaders requires insight from indigenous women researchers in addition to critical others in the field. Similarly, Curtis (2014) argues that research on 'race' and leadership, especially where Black women are included, enables 'new voices' to emerge while 'sharing absent realities'. As this diversity benefits the academy while challenging its dominant epistemologies, Black women's experiences become part of the leadership narrative that is valued. White (2010) is an example of how inclusive research on leadership can further our knowledge of diverse leadership experiences while recognising the political contract necessary for such work to be conducted.

On this note, the paucity of literature on Black leaders in sport leaves in the shadows the skills developed by them that enable the navigation of systems that unfairly constrain and disempower. These competences and experiences should not be under-valued or ignored. In the interests of social justice and effective leadership, stakeholders in sport that include activist scholars, policy makers and practitioners should be required to augment their understanding and adherence to these important concerns. These issues resonate with the imperative to develop culturally sensitive research, as outlined in Chapter 3 where the biographies of White researchers revealed a labrynthine task of reflection/reflexion and political standpoints required to conduct critical research on 'race'. These positions did not necessarily improve the representation of Black researchers in the academy but utilised White identities, privilege and informed standpoints with the aim of disrupting racial hierarchies, discrimination and oppression in sport and leisure research.

The colour line remains a twenty-first-century concern that has been consistently established through the way racism has remained embedded in society. The challenges ahead for our theory, policy and practice in sport are no less significant today than in previous generations. Though the challenges today might be similar to those in the past they remain fluid, differently organised online and offline and generally more covert. Critical Race Theory remains a thought-provoking and pragmatic framework for activist scholars. Its architecture, defined by common tenets outlined in Chapter 1, is foundational to critiques that centre 'race', racism and their impacts on sport and society. CRT's focus on transformation rather than liberal incrementalism guards against critique for critique's sake. Past and present racial processes and formations that require disruption remain the point of departure in social arenas like sport, whose influence has the potential to transform dysfunctional social arrangements.

REFERENCES

Ackerman, N. (2014, 9 October). Jose Mourinho blasted for racism stance by FIFA vice-president Jeffrey Webb. Retrieved 10 October 2014, from http://bleacherreport.com/arti cles/2225671-jose-mourinho-blasted-for-racism-stance-by-fifa-vice-president-jeffrey-webb

Agencies (2013). Paolo Di Canio hits back at 'stupid and ridiculous' racism accusation. *Guardian*, 1 April.

Agyemang, K. and J. Singer (2014). Race in the present day: NBA employees sound off on race and racism. *Journal of African American Studies* 18: 11–32.

Ahmed, S. (2006). The nonperformativity of antiracism. *Meridians: Feminism, Race, Transnationalism* 7(1): 104–126.

Aleman, S. and E. Aleman (2016). Critical race media projects: counterstories and praxis (re) claim Chicana/o experiences. *Urban Education* 5(3): 287–314.

Alexander, C. and J. Arday (2015). *Aiming higher: race, inequality and diversity in the academy*. Runnymede Perspectives. London, Runnymede Trust: 1–48.

Alexander, H. (2015). What is going wrong in France's prisons? *Telegraph*, 17 January.

Amara, M. and I. Henry (2010). Sport, Muslim identities and cultures in the UK: an emerging policy issue: case studies of Leicester and Birmingham. *European Sport Management Quarterly* 10(4): 419–443.

Anderson, P. (2015). Sporting women and Machonas: negotiating gender through sports in Argentina, 1900–1946. *Women's History Review* 24(5): 700–720.

Andrews, J. and G. Andrews (2003). Life in a secure unit: the rehabilitation of young people through the use of sport. *Social Science and Medicine* 56(1): 531–550.

Andronoviene, L. (2014). The practice of humour and our spirituality: some reflections. *Journal of European Baptist Studies* 14(3): 22–33.

Annamma, S., Connor, D. and Ferri, B. (2013). Dis/ability critical race studies (DisCrit): theorizing at the intersections of race and dis/ability. *Race, Ethnicity and Education* 16(1): 1–31.

Anthias, F. and N. Yuval-Davis (1993). *Racialized boundaries*. London, Routledge.

Apple, M. (1998). Foreword. In: *White reign: deploying whiteness in America*, eds J. Kincheloe, S. Steinberg, N. Rodriguez and R. Chennault. New York, St. Martin's Griffin.

Arai, S. and B. Kivel (2009). Critical race theory and social justice perspectives on whiteness, difference(s) and (anti)racism: a fourth wave of race research in leisure studies. *Journal of Leisure Research* 41(4): 459–470.

Ashe, A. (1993). *Days of grace*. London, Heinemann.

Association, P. (2013). Paolo Di Canio is 'mad as a hatter', says Trevor Sinclair. *Guardian*, 4 April.

Back, L. (2001). The white fortresses in cyberspace. *Unesco Courier* (January): 44–46.

Badenhausen, K. (2012). Tiger Woods delivered $6 million more for sponsors than Rory McIlroy In 2012. Retrieved 10 January 2013, from www.forbes.com/sites/kurtbadenha usen/2012/11/29/tiger-woods-delivered-6-million-more-for-sponsors-than-rory-m cilroy-in-2012/

Bandyopadhyay, M. (2006). Competing masculinities in a prison. *Men and Masculinities* 9(2): 186–203.

Battiste, M. (2007). Researching ethics for protecting Indigenous knowledge and heritage: institutional and researcher responsibilities. In: *Ethical Futures in Qualitative Research*, eds N. Denzin and M. D. Giardina. Walnut Creek CA, Left Coast Press: 111–132.

Bell, D. (1980). Brown v. Board of Education and the interest convergence dilemma. *Harvard Law Review* 93: 518–533.

Bell, D. (1992). *Faces at the bottom of the well: the permanence of racism*. New York, Basic Books.

Bell, D. (1995). Who's afraid of critical race theory? *University of Illinois Law Review* 893: 893–910.

Berger, A. (1995). *Blind men and elephants: perspectives on humour*. New Brunswick NJ, Transaction Publications.

Berger, A. (2013). Forty-five ways to make 'em laugh. *Israeli Journal of Humor Research* 3 (June).

Berman, G. and A. Dar (2013). *Prison population statistics*. London, House of Commons.

Bhattacharya, T. (2017). Donald Trump: the unanticipated apotheosis of neoliberalism. *Cultural Dynamics* 29(1–2): 108–116.

Black Girls Do Bike (2017). Black girls do bike. Retrieved 1 August 2017, from www.bla ckgirlsdobike.com/home

Blair, M. (1998). The myth of neutrality in educational research. In: *Researching Racism in Education*, eds P. Connell and B. Troyna. Buckingham, Open University Press: 12–20.

Blaisdell, B. (2009). *Seeing with poetic eyes: critical race theory and moving from liberal to critical forms of race research in the sociology of education*. Rotterdam, Sense Publishers.

Bloom, J. (2017). 'To die for a lousy bike': bicycles, race, and the regulation of public space on the streets of Washington, DC, 1963–2009. *American Quarterly* 69(1): 47–70.

Bonilla-Silva, E. (2006). *Racism without racists: color-blind racism and the persistence of racial inequality in the United States*. Lanham MD and Oxford, Rowman & Littlefield.

Bonilla-Silva, E. (2010). *Racism without racists: color-blind racism and the persistence of racial inequality in the United States*. Lanham MD and Oxford, Rowman & Littlefield.

Borland, J. and J. Bruening (2010). Navigating barriers: a qualitative examination of the under-representation of Black females as head coaches in collegiate basketball. *Sport Management Review* 13: 407–420.

Bosman, J. and M. Smith (2017). Chicago Police routinely trampled on civil rights, Justice Dept. says. *New York Times*, 13 January.

Boutros, A. (2015). Religion in the Afrosphere: the constitution of a blogging counter-public. *Journal of Communication Inquiry* 39(4): 319–337.

Bowers, M. (2005). 'Ethnic glue': humour in Native American literatures. In: *Cheeky fictions: laughter and the postcolonial*, eds S. Reichl and M. Stein. Amsterdam, Rodopi.

Bowleg, L. (2008). When black + lesbian + woman ≠ black lesbian woman: the methodological challenges of qualitative and quantitative intersectionality research. *Sex Roles* 59: 312–325.

Bradbury, S., Amara, M., García, B. and Bairner, A. (2011). *Representation and structural discrimination in football in Europe: the case of minorities and women – summary report of key findings*. Leicester, Institute of Youth Sport/Loughborough University.

Bradbury, S., Van Sterkenburg, J. and Mignon, P. (2015). *The glass ceiling in European football: levels of representation of visible ethnic minorities and women in leadership positions, and the experiences of elite level ethnic minority coaches*. www.farenet.org/, FARE: 1–20.

Bramham, P. (2002). Rojek, the sociological imagination and leisure. *Leisure Studies* 21(3/4): 221–234.

Bridgewater, S. (2014). How are football coaches appointed? www.farenet.org/, League Managers' Association.

Brohm, J. (1989). *Sport: a prison of measured time*. Worcester, Billing and Sons Ltd.

Bruno Massao, P. and K. Fasting (2014). Mapping race, class and gender: experiences from Black Norwegian athletes. *European Journal for Sport and Society* 11(4): 331–352.

Burdsey, D. (2004). 'One of the lads': dual ethnicity and assimilated ethnicities in the careers of British Asian professional footballers. *Ethnic and Racial Studies* 27(5): 757–779.

Burdsey, D. (2011a). Applying a CRT lens to sport in the UK: the case of professional football. In: *Atlantic Crossings: International Dialogues on Critical Race Theory*, eds K. Hylton, A. Pilkington, P. Warmington and S. Housee. Birmingham, Higher Education Academy Network.

Burdsey, D. (2011b). That joke isn't funny anymore: racial microaggressions, colour-blind ideology and the mitigation of racism in English men's first class cricket. *Sociology of Sport Journal* 28: 261–283.

Burdsey, D., Thangaraj, S. and Dudrah, R. (2013). Playing through time and space: sport and South Asian diasporas. *South Asian Popular Culture* 11(3): 211–218.

Burkhalter, B. (1999). Reading race online: discovering racial identity in Usenet discussions. In: *Communities in Cyberspace*, eds M. Smith and P. Kollock. London, Routledge: 60–75.

Burns, T. (1992). *Erving Goffman*. London, Routledge.

Burton, L. and S. Leberman (2015). Diversity in sport leadership. In: *Leadership in sport*, eds I. Boyle, D. Murray and P. Cummins. London, Routledge.

Business in the Community (2015). *Race at work*. London, Business in the Community.

Butler Trust (2014, 9 October). Transforming prisons and prisoners through physical education. Retrieved 20 December 2016, from www.butlertrust.org.uk/transforming-prisons-prisoners-through-physical-education/

Carrington, B. (2010). *Race, sport and politics*. London, Sage.

Carrington, B. (2012). Introduction: sport matters. *Ethnic and Racial Studies* 35(6): 961–970.

Carrington, B. (2013). The critical sociology of race and sport: the first 50 years. *Annual Review of Sociology* 39: 379–398.

Carter-Francique, A., Lawrence, S. and Eyanson, C. (2011). African american female athletes' stories about race: a phenomenological exploration. *Journal of Global Intelligence and Policy* 4(4): 1–18.

CCRC (2003). Critical race theory. Canadian Critical Race Conference: Pedagogy and Practice, University of British Columbia.

Charmaz, K. (2005). Grounded theory in the 21st century. In: *Sage handbook of qualitative research*, eds N. Denzin and Y. Lincoln. London, Sage: 507–535.

Chicago Police Accountability Task Force Community Forum (2016). Chicago Police Community Forum. https://chicagopatf.org/events/

Childers-McKee, C. and K. Hytten (2015). Critical race feminism and the complex challenges of educational reform. *Urban Review* 47: 393–412.

Christian, M. (2011). Mixing up the game: social and historical contours of black mixed heritage players in British football. *In: Race, ethnicity and football: persisting debates and emergent issues*, ed. D. Burdsey. London, Routledge.

Clarke, L. (1998). Commentary. *Journal of Psychiatry and Mental Health Nursing* 5: 319–328.

Cleland, J. and E. Cashmore (2014). Fans, racism and British football in the twenty-first century: the existence of a 'colour-blind' ideology. *Journal of Ethnic and Migration Studies* 40(4): 638–654.

Cleland, J. and E. Cashmore (2016). Football fans' views of racism in British football. *International Review for the Sociology of Sport* 51(1): 27–43.

CNN (2013). CNN FC: PSG's gamble on David Beckham/FIFA Fighting Racism. 15 September. www.cnn.com/videos/sports/2013/03/22/football-club-beckham-wright-brassell.cnn

Coalter, F. (2007). *A wider social role for sport*. London, Routledge.

Coram, S. and C. Hallinan (2017). Critical race theory and the orthodoxy of race neutrality: examining the denigration of Adam Goodes. *Australian Aboriginal Studies* 1: 99–111.

Council of Europe (2012). *Young People combatting hate speech online*. Strasbourg, Council of Europe.

Coyle, A. (2009). *A human rights approach to prison management: handbook for prison staff*. London, King's College London International Centre for Prison Studies.

CRE (2003). *Racial equality in prisons*. London, Commission for Racial Equality.

Crenshaw, K., Gotanda, N., Peller, G. and Thomas, K., eds (1995). *Critical race theory: the key writings that formed the movement*. New York, New Press.

Critchley, S. (2002). *On humour*. London, Routledge.

Cummings, A. (2010). Furious kinship: critical race theory and the hip-hop nation. *University of Louisville Law Review* 48: 499–577.

Cunningham, G. (2010). Understanding the under-representation of African American coaches: a multilevel perspective. *Sport Management Review* 13(4): 395–406.

Cunningham, G. (2011). Does diversity in sport reduce racial prejudice? *In: Sport and Challenges to racism*, eds J. Long and K. Spracklen. London, Palgrave Macmillan.

Cunningham, G., Miner, D. and McDonald, J. (2012). Being different and suffering the consequences: the influence of head coach–player racial dissimilarity on experienced incivility. *International Review for the Sociology of Sport* 48(6): 689–705.

Curtis, S. (2014). Black women leaders in early years education. Ph.D. dissertation, School of Education, Carnegie Faculty, Leeds Metropolitan University.

Davey, M. and M. Smith (2016). Chicago Police Dept. plagued by systemic racism, task force finds. *New York Times*, 13 April.

Dávila, B. (2015). Critical race theory, disability microaggressions and Latina/o student experiences in special education. *Race, Ethnicity and Education* 18(4).

Davis, A. (2001). Race, gender, and prison history: from the convict lease system to the supermax prison. *In: Prison masculinities*, eds D. Sabo, T. Kupers and W. London. Philadelphia, Temple University Press.

Delgado, R. (1995). Storytelling for oppositionists and others: a plea for a narrative. *In: Critical race theory: the cutting edge*, eds R. Delgado and J. Stefancic. Philadelphia, Temple University Press: 60–70.

Delgado, R., ed. (2012). *Critical race theory: the cutting edge*. Philadelphia, Temple University Press.

Delgado, R. and J. Stefancic (1995). Why do we tell the same stories? Law reform, critical librarianship, and the triple helix dilemma. *In: Critical race theory: the cutting edge*, eds R. Delgado and J. Stefancic. Philadelphia, Temple University Press: 206–216.

Delgado, R. and J. Stefancic (1997). *Critical white studies: looking behind the mirror*. Philadelphia, Temple University Press.

Delgado, R. and J. Stefancic (1999). *Critical race theory: the cutting edge*. Philadelphia, Temple University Press.

Delgado, R. and J. Stefancic (2001). *Critical race theory: an introduction*. New York, New York University Press.

Delgado, R. and J. Stefancic (2012). *Critical race theory: an introduction*. New York, New York University Press.

Diette, T. (2013). Brown v. Board of Education. *In: Encyclopedia of race and racism*, ed. P. Mason. Michigan, Gale: 2: 320–326.

Dixson, A. D. and C. K. Rousseau (2005). And we are still not saved: critical race theory in education ten years later. *Race, Ethnicity and Education* 8(1): 7–27.

Dixson, A. D. and C. K. Rousseau (2006). *Critical race theory in education: all God's children got a song*. New York and London, Routledge.

Donath, J. (1999). Identity and deception in the virtual community. *In: Communities in cyberspace*, eds M. Smith and P. Kollock. London, Routledge: 29–59.

Dorsey, J. (2016). *The turbulent world of Middle East soccer*. London, Hurst and Company.

Dovidio, J. (1993). The subtlety of racism. *Training and Development* (April): 51–57.

Dovidio, J. and S. Gaertner (2000). Aversive racism and selection decisions: 1989 and 1999. *Psychological Science* 11(4): 315–319.

Du Bois, W. E. B. (1920). *Darkwater: voices from within the veil*. New York, Harcourt, Brace and Company.

Du Bois, W. E. B. (1994). *The souls of Black folk*. New York, Dover Publications.

Du Bois, W. E. B. (1998). *Black reconstruction in America 1860–1880*. New York, The Free Press.

Duff, M. (2005). Football's fascist salute row. Retrieved 12 August 2016, from http://news.bbc.co.uk/1/hi/world/europe/4158591.stm

Duru, J. N. (2011). *Advancing the ball: race, reformation and the quest for equal opportunity in the NFL*. New York, Oxford University Press.

Duster, T., Twine Warren, J. W. and Winddance, F. (1999). *Race-ing research, researching race: methodological dilemmas in critical race studies*. New York, New York University Press

Earle, R. and C. Phillips (2013). 'Muslim is the new black': new ethnicities and new essentialisms in the prison. *Race and Justice* 3(2): 114–129.

Edinburgh Festival of Cycling (2017). The Quick Brown Fox: an evening with Ayesha McGowan. Retrieved 1 August 2017, from https://edfoc.org.uk/events/event/quick-brown-fox-evening-ayesha-mcgowan/

Edwards, H. (1979). Sport within the veil: the triumphs, tragedies and challenges of Afro-American involvement. *Annals of the American Academy of Political and Social Science* 445 (September): 116–127.

Elliot, J. (2016). Speaks volumes: anti racism activist and educator Jane Elliot speaks to White citizens on receiving the same treatment as Black citizens. Available at kilsai.rihan.ru/1

Ellison, R. (1965). *Invisible man*. St Ives, Penguin.

Epp, C. and M. Maynard-Moody (2014). Driving while black. *Washington Monthly*, January/February.

Epp, C. and M. Maynard-Moody (2016). Philando Castile and the human costs of a widespread police practice. *Washington Monthly*, 21 July.

Equality Challenge Unit (2013). *Unconscious bias and higher education*. London, ECU.

Fanon, F. (1967). *Black skin, white masks*. New York, Grove Press.

Farrington, N., Hall, L., Kilvington, D., Price, J. and Saeed, A. (2015). *Sport, racism and social media*. London, Routledge.

Farrington, N., Kilvington, D., Price, J. and Saeed, A. (2012). *Race, racism and sports journalism*. London, Routledge.

Feagin, J. (2010). *The white racial frame: centuries of racial framing and counter-framing*. London, Routledge.

Feagin, J. and K. McKinney (2003). *The many costs of racism*. Lanham MD, Rowman & Littlefield.

Ferguson, D. (2011). PGA tour and European tour chiefs say Woods-Williams case closed. *PGA News Archive*, 2 November.

Fine, M. (2004). Witnessing whiteness/gathering intelligence. In: *Off white: readings on power, privilege, and resistance*, eds M. Fine, L. Weis, L. Powell Pruitt and A. Burns. New York, Routledge.

Fine, M., Weis, L., Weseen, S. and Wong, L. (2003). For whom? Qualitative research, representations and social responsibilities. In: *The landscape of qualitative research*, eds N. Denzin and Y. Lincoln. London, Sage.

Fitzpatrick, K. and L. J. Santamaría (2015). Disrupting racialization: considering critical leadership in the field of physical education. *Physical Education and Sport Pedagogy* 20(5): 532–546.

Fletcher, T. (2014). 'Does he look like a Paki?' An exploration of 'whiteness'. positionality and reflexivity in inter-racial sports research. *Qualitative Research in Sport, Exercise and Health* 6(2): 244–260.

Fletcher, T. and K. Hylton (2017). 'Race', whiteness and sport. In: *Routledge handbook of sport, race and ethnicity*, eds J. Nauright and D. Wiggins. London, Routledge.

Fletcher, T. and K. Hylton (forthcoming 2017). Whiteness in event organisation. *Journal for Policy Research in Tourism, Leisure and Events*.

Fletcher, T., Piggot, D., North, J. K. H., Gilbert, S. and Norman, L. (2014). *Exploring the barriers to South Asian cricket players' entry and progression in coaching*. Leeds, England and Wales Cricket Board: 53.

Flintoff, A., Dowling, F. and Fitzgerald, H. (2014). Working through whiteness, race and (anti) racism in physical education teacher education. *Physical Education and Sport Pedagogy* 11(3): 247–263.

Ford, C. L. and C. O. Airhihenbuwa (2010). Critical race theory, race equity, and public health: toward antiracism praxis. *American Journal of Public Health* 100(SI): 30–35.

Ford, T., Richardson, K. and Petit, W. (2015). Disparagement humor and prejudice: contemporary theory and research. *Humor* 28(2): 171–186.

Fortune, D. and C. Whyte (2011). Re-imagining institutional spaces: the communitizing potential of leisure. *Leisure/Loisir* 35(1): 19–35.

Foxton, W. (2012). Google denies racial profiling via Gmail: here are some disturbing questions it still needs to answer. *Daily Telegraph*, 4 September.

Freud, S. (1991 [1960]). *Jokes and their relation to the unconscious*. New York, Penguin.

Gabbidon, S. and H. Taylor Greene (2005). *Race and crime*. London, Sage.

Gaertner, S. and J. Dovidio (2005). Understanding and addressing contemporary racism: from aversive racism to common ingroup identity model. *Journal of Social Issues* 611(3): 615–639.

Gaggiano, A. (2005). Using a comic vision to contend with tragedy: three unusual African English novels. In: *Cheeky fictions: laughter and the postcolonial*, eds S. Reichl and M. Stein. Amsterdam, Rodopi.

Gallagher, C. A. (2000). White like me? In: *Race-ing research, researching race: methodological dilemmas in critical race studies*, eds F. Winddance Twine and J. Warren. New York, New York University Press: 67–92.

Garner, S. (2007). *Whiteness: an introduction*. Abingdon, Routledge.

Giardina, M. D. (2003). 'Bending it like Beckham' in the global popular: stylish hybridity, performativity, and the politics of representation. *Journal of Sport and Social Issues* 27(1): 65–82.

Giddens, A. (1984). *The constitution of society*. Cambridge, Polity Press.

Gillborn, D. (2006). Critical race theory beyond North America. In: *Critical race theory in education: all God's children got a song*, eds A. D. Dixson and C. K. Rousseau. New York, Routledge.

Gillborn, D. (2008). *Racism and education: coincidence or conspiracy?* London, Routledge.

Gillborn, D. (2009). *Racism and education: coincidence or conspiracy?* London, Routledge.

Gillborn, D. (2011). Once upon a time in the UK: race, class, hope and whiteness in the academy (personal reflections on the birth of 'BritCrit'). In: *Atlantic crossings: international dialogues on critical race theory*, eds K. Hylton, A. Pilkington, P. Warmington and S. Housee. Birmingham, CSAP/Higher Education Academy.

Gillborn, D. (2016). White lies: things we're told about race and education that aren't true. Leeds Beckett Annual Race Lecture. Leeds, Leeds Beckett University.

Glover, K. S. (2009). *Racial profiling: research, racism, and resistance*. Lanham MD, Rowman & Littlefield.

Glynn, M. (2014). *Black men, invisibility and desistance from crime: towards a critical race theory of desistance*. London, Routledge.

Goffman, E. (1959). *The presentation of self in everyday life*. London, Penguin.

Goffman, E. (1961). *Asylums: essays on the social situations of mental patients and other inmates*. Garden City NY, Anchor Books.

Gold, S. (2016). A critical race theory approach to black American entrepreneurship. *Ethnic and Racial Studies* 39(9): 1697–1718.

Goldberg, D. T. (2008). Racisms without racism. *PMLA (Journal of the Modern Language Association of America)* 123(5): 1712–1716.

Goldberg, D. T. (2015). *Are we all post-racial yet? Debating race*. Cambridge, Polity Press.

Gratton, C. and I. Jones (2004). *Research methods for sport studies*. London, Routledge.

Green, J., Steinbach, R., Datta, J. and Edwards, P. (2010). *Cycling in London: a study of social and cultural factors in transport mode choice. A final report to the Smarter Travel Unit, Transport for London*. London, London School of Hygiene and Tropical Medicine.

Guardian (2013). Chris Powell says of Paolo Di Canio's politics: 'You'll have to ask him'. *Guardian*, 3 April.

Guardian Sport (2017). 'I'm black so I look mean?' Serena Williams discusses race and pregnancy. *Guardian*, 15 August.

Guinier, L. and G. Torres (2003). *The miner's canary: enlisting race, resisting power, transforming democracy*. Cambridge MA, Harvard University Press.

Gunaratnam, Y. (2003). *Researching 'race' and ethnicity: methods, knowledge and power*. London, Sage.

Gunn Allen, P. (1992). *The sacred hoop*. Boston, Beacon Press.

Hall, M. (1998). Africa connected. *First Monday.Org* 3(11): 1–12.

Harris, C. and L. Kyle-DeBose (2007). *Charging the net: a history of Blacks in tennis from Althea Gibson and Arthur Ashe to the Williams sisters*. Chicago, Ivan R. Dee.

Harris, D. (1997). 'Driving while Black' and all other traffic offences: the Supreme Court and pretextual traffic stops. *Journal of Criminal Law and Criminology* 87(2): 544–582.

Harrison, A. K. (2013). Black skiing, everyday racism, and the racial spatiality of whiteness. *Journal of Sport and Social Issues* 37(4): 315–339.

Harrison, L., Azzarito, L. and Burden, J. (2004). Perceptions of athletic superiority: a view from the other side. *Race, Ethnicity and Education* 7(2): 159–166.

Harrison, L., Carson, R. and Burden, J. (2010). Physical education teachers' cultural competency. *Journal of Teaching in Physical Education* 29: 184–198.

Hawkins, B., Carter-Francique, A. and Cooper, J. N., eds (2017). *Critical race theory: black athletic sporting experiences in the United States*. New York, Palgrave Macmillan.

Hill Collins, P. and S. Bilge (2016). *Intersectionality*. Cambridge, Polity Press.

Hogg, M. (2001). A social identity theory of leadership. *Personality and Social Psychology Review* 5(3): 184–200.

Holland, B. (1997). Surviving leisure time racism: the burden of racial harassment on Britain's black footballers. *Leisure Studies* 16: 261–277.

Holland, S. P. (2012). *The erotic life of racism*. Durham NC, Duke University Press.

Holmes, M. D. and B. W. Smith (2008). *Race and police brutality: roots of an urban dilemma*. Albany NY, SUNY Press. Distributed in Britain by University Presses Marketing, Bristol.

hooks, b. (1989). *Talking back: thinking feminist, thinking black*. Boston, South End Press.

hooks, b. (1999). Whiteness in the black imagination. *In: Displacing whiteness: essays in social and cultural criticism*, ed. R. Frankenburg. Durham NC, Duke University Press: 165–179.

Howard Griffin, J. (2010). *Black like me*. San Antonio TX, Wings Press.

Hughey, M. (2011). Backstage discourse and the reproduction of white masculinities. *Sociological Quarterly* 52(1): 132–153.

Hutnyk, J. (1997). Adorno at Womad: South Asian crossovers and the limits of hybridity-talk. *In: Debating cultural hybridity: multi-cultural identities and the politics of anti-racism*, eds P. Werbner and T. Modood. London, Zed Books.

Huxley, M. (2015). Adam Goodes should apologise, says mother of girl who called him an ape. *Guardian*, 29 July.

Hylton, K. (2003). *Local government, 'race' and sports policy implementation: demystifying equal opportunities in local government*. Leeds, Leeds Metropolitan University: iv.

Hylton, K. (2005). 'Race', sport and leisure: lessons from critical race theory. *Leisure Studies* 24(1): 81–98.

Hylton, K. (2009). *'Race' and sport: critical race theory*. London, Routledge.

Hylton, K. (2010). How a turn to critical race theory can contribute to our understanding of 'race', racism and anti-racism in sport. *International Review for the Sociology of Sport* 45(3): 335–354.

Hylton, K. (2012). Talk the talk, walk the walk: defining critical race theory in research. *Race, Ethnicity and Education* 15(1): 23–41.

Hylton, K. (2015). 'Race' talk! tensions and contradictions in sport and PE. *Physical Education and Sport Pedagogy* 20(5): 503–516.

Hylton, K. (2015). This way … this explains my reality: critical race theory in sport and leisure. *In: Routledge handbook of theory in sport management*, eds J. Fink, A. Doherty and G. Cunningham. New York, Routledge.

Hylton, K. (2016). Racism affects both sports stars and their communities. Retrieved 16 August 2016, from www.sbs.com.au/nitv/article/2016/02/04/racism-affects-both-sports-stars-and-their-communities.

Hylton, K. (2017a). The unbearable whiteness of cycling. *The Conversation*, 27 April. www.the conversation.com

Hylton, K. (2017b) Expert Opinion 'The Unbearable Whiteness of Cycling', Cycling Weekly. Thursday August 24th, pp39.

Hylton, K. and S. Lawrence (2015). Reading Ronaldo: contingent whiteness in the football media. *Soccer and Society* 16(5/6): 765–782.

Hylton, K. and S. Lawrence (2016). 'For your ears only!' Donald Sterling and backstage racism in sport. *Ethnic and Racial Studies*, online at www.tandfonline.com, 11 March, 1–18. Also vol. 39(15): 2740–2757.

Hylton, K. and J. Long (2016). Confronting 'race' and policy: 'how can you research something you say does not exist?' *Journal of Policy Research in Tourism, Leisure and Events* 8(1–3): 202–208.

Hylton, K. and J. Long (2017). 'Knowing me, knowing you': biographies and subjectivities in the study of 'race'. In: *Sport, leisure and social justice*, eds J. Long, T. Fletcher and R. Watson. London, Routledge.

Hylton, K. and N. D. Morpeth (2012). London 2012: 'race' matters, and the East End. *International Journal of Sport Policy and Politics* 4(2): 1–18.

Hylton, K. and N. D. Morpeth (2014). 'Race' matters, and the east end. In: *The 'Olympic and Paralympic' effect on public policy*, eds D. Boyce and A. Smith. London, Routledge.

Hylton, K., Pilkington, A., Warmington, P. and Housee, S., eds (2011). *Atlantic crossings: international dialogues on critical race theory*. Birmingham, CSAP/Higher Education Academy.

Hylton, K. and A. J. Rankin (2016). 'Race', sport, and politics. In: *Handbook of sport and politics*, eds A. Bairner, J. Kelly and J. W. Lee. London, Routledge.

Hynes, M. and S. Scott (2015). Black-faced, red faces: the potentials of humour for anti-racist action. *Ethnic and Racial Studies*, online at www.tandfonline.com, 23 November, 1–18. Also vol. 39(1): 87–104.

Ignatiev, N. (1997). The point is not to interpret whiteness but to abolish it. Talk given at the conference 'The Making and Unmaking of Whiteness', Berkeley, California, 11–13 April 1997.

IOC (2017). IOC takes a stand against discrimination and celebrates the power of sport to fight racism. Retrieved 25 August, from https://www.olympic.org/news/ioc-takes-a-stand-against-discrimination-and-celebrates-the-power-of-sport-to-fightracism

Irwin, M. (2011). Ashley Cole: I didn't hear John Terry make any racist comments. *The Sun*, 26 October.

Jean, Y. and J. Feagin (1998). *Double burden: Black women and everyday racism*. New York, Routledge.

Jewkes, Y. (2005). Men behind bars: 'doing' masculinity as an adaptation to imprisonment. *Men and Masculinities* 8(1): 44–63.

Jones, R. L. (2002). The Black experience within English semiprofessional soccer. *Journal of Sport and Social Issues* 26(1): 47–66.

Kang, J. (2003). Cyber-race. In: *AsianAmerican.Net: ethnicity, nationalism, and cyberspace*, eds R. Lee and S. C. Wong. London, Routledge.

Kazemian, K. and C. Andersson (2012). *The French prison system: comparative insights for policy and practice in New York and the United States*. New York, Research and Evaluation Center: 1–29.

Keeley, G. (2008). I am not a racist, says Spanish F1 fan who 'blacked-up' for Hamilton. *Independent*, 8 February.

Kick it Out (2016). Kick it Out unveils findings of research into football related hate crime on social media. www.kickitout.org/get-involved/report-it/kick-it-out-unveils-findings-of-research-into-football-related-hate-crime-on-social-media/

Kick it Out (2016). Klick it Out campaign: the findings. Retrieved 4 September 2016, from www.kickitout.org/news/klick-it-out-campaign-the-findings/

King, C. (2004). *Offside racism: playing the white man*. Oxford, Berg.

King, C. R. (2006). Defacements/effacements: anti-Asian (American) sentiment in sport. *Journal of Sport and Social Issues* 30(4): 340–352.

King, J. E. (1997). Dysconscious racism: ideology, identity, and miseducation. In: *Critical white studies: looking behind the mirror*, eds R. Delgado and J. Stefancic. Philadelphia, Temple University Press: 128–135.

Klugman, M. and G. Osmond (2013). *Black and proud*. Sydney, New South Publishing.

Kovel, J. (1970). *White racism: a psychohistory*. [S.l.]. New York, Pantheon.

Krasovic, T. (2016). Colin Kaepernick takes a knee during national anthem in San Diego and is booed. *Los Angeles Times*, 1 September.

Ladson-Billings, G. (1998). Just What is Critical Race Theory, and What's it Doing in a *Nice* Field Like education? *Qualitative Studies in Education*, 11, 7–24.

Ladson-Billings, G. and W. F. Tate IV (2006). Toward a critical race theory of education. *In: All God's children got a song*, eds A. D. Dixson and C. K. Rousseau. New York, Routledge.

Lawrence, S. (2014). Racialising the 'great man': a critical race study of idealised male athletic bodies in Men's Health magazine. *International Review for the Sociology of Sport* 51(7): 777–799.

Lawrence, S. M. and B. D. Tatum (2004). White educators as allies: moving from awareness to action. *In: Off white: readings on power, privilege and resistance*, eds M. Fine, L. Weis, L. P. Pruitt and A. Burns. London, Routledge.

Leicester, J. (2011). By not acting golf flunks own racism test. Associated Press, 9 November.

Leonard, J. (2000). *A course of their own: a history of African American golfer*. Kansas City, Stark Books.

Leonardo, Z., ed. (2005). *Critical pedagogy and race*. Malden MA, Blackwell.

Leonardo, Z. (2009). *Race, whiteness, and education*. New York and London, Routledge.

Leung, L. (2005). *Virtual ethnicity: race, resistance and the World Wide Web*. Aldershot, Ashgate.

Lockyer, S. and M. Pickering, eds (2005). *Beyond a joke: the limits of humour*. Basingstoke, Palgrave Macmillan.

Logan, N. (2011). The White leader prototype: a critical analysis of race in public relations. *Journal of Public Relations Research* 23(4): 442–457.

Long, J., Fletcher, T. and Watson, B., eds (2017). *Sport, leisure and social justice: critical perspectives on equality and social justice in sport and leisure*. London, Routledge.

Long, J. and K. Hylton (2002). Shades of white: an examination of whiteness in sport. *Leisure Studies* 21(1): 87–103.

Long, J., Hylton, K., Ratna, A., Spracklen, K. and Bailey, S. (2009). *A systematic review of the literature on Black and minority ethnic communities in sport and physical recreation*. Birmingham, Sporting Equals.

Long, J., Hylton, K. and Spracklen, K. (2014). Whiteness, blackness and settlement: leisure and the integration of new migrants. *Journal of Ethnic and Migration Studies* 40(11): 1779–1797.

Long, J., Hylton, K., Welch, M. and Dart, J. (2000). *Part of the game: an examination of the nature and extent of racism in grass roots football*. London, Kick it Out.

Long, J. and I. Sanderson (2001). The social benefits of sport: where's the proof? *In: Sport in the city*, eds C. Gratton and I. Henry. London, Routledge: 187–203.

Long, J. and K. Spracklen, eds (2011). *Sport and challenges to racism*. London, Routledge.

Lorenz, S. and R. Murray (2014). 'Goodbye to the gangstas': the NBA dress code, Ray Emery, and the policing of blackness in basketball and hockey. *Journal of Sport and Social Issues* 38(1): 23–50.

Luscombe, B. (2014). Harvard study suggests racial bias among some Airbnb renters. *Health and Time*, 27 January: 1.

Lusted, J. (2009). Playing games with 'race': understanding resistance to 'race' equality initiatives in English local football governance. *Soccer and Society* 10(6): 722–739.

Lynn, M. (2005). Critical race theory, Afrocentricity, and their relationship to critical pedagogy. *In: Critical pedagogy and race*, ed. Z. Leonardo. Oxford, Blackwell: 127–169.

Macpherson, S. W. o. C. (1999). *Report of the Stephen Lawrence Inquiry*. London, HMSO.

Malik, K. (1996). *The meaning of race*. Basingstoke, Macmillan.

Marqusee, M. (1995). Sport and stereotype: from role model to Muhammad Ali. *Race and Class* 36(4): 1–29.

Martos-Garcia, D., Devis-Devis, J. and Sparkes, A. (2009). Sport and physical activity in a high security Spanish prison: an ethnographic study of multiple meanings. *Sport, Education and Society* 14(1): 77–96.

Matsuda, M. J., Lawrence, C. R., Delgado, R. and Crenshaw, K. W. (1993). *Words that wound: critical race theory, assaultive speech, and the First Amendment*. Boulder CO, Westview Press.

McIntosh, P. (1988). *White privilege and male privilege: a personal account of coming to see correspondences through work in women's studies*. Wellesley MA, Wellesley College Centre for Research on Women.

McKinley, B. and J. Brayboy (2006). Toward a tribal critical race theory in education. *The Urban Review* 37(5): 425–446.

McNair, J. (2008). 'I may be crackin', but um fackin': racial humour in *The Watson's Go to Birmingham – 1963*. *Children's Literature in Education* 39: 201–212.

Meek, R. (2014). *Sport in prison: exploring the role of physical activity in correctional settings*. London, Routledge.

Meek, R. and N. Champion (2012). *Fit for release*. Mitcham, Prisoners Education Trust.

Meek, R. and G. Lewis (2012). The role of sport in promoting prisoner health. *International Journal of Prisoner Health* 8(3/4): 117–130.

Meek, R. and G. Lewis (2014). The impact of a sports initiative for young men in prison: staff and participant perspectives. *Journal of Sport and Social Issues* 38(2): 95–123.

Meer, S. (2005). *Uncle Tom mania: slavery, minstrelsy and transatlatic culture in the 1850s*. Athens GA and London, University of Georgia Press.

Messner, M. A. and D. F. Sabo (1990). *Sport, men, and the gender order: critical feminist perspectives*. Champaign IL, Human Kinetics.

Mills, C. (1970). *The sociological imagination*. London, Oxford University Press.

Mills, C. (2007). White ignorance. *In: Race and epistemologies of ignorance*, eds S. Sullivan and N. Tuana. Albany, State University of New York Press: 12–38.

Ministry of Justice (2015). *Associations between ethnic background and being sentenced to prison in the crown court in England and Wales in 2015*. London, Ministry of Justice.

Ministry of Justice (2016). *National Offender Management Service offender equalities annual report 2015/16*. London, National Offender Management Service, Ministry of Justice.

Ministry of Justice (2016). *Statistics on women and the criminal justice system 2015*. London, National Offender Management Service, Ministry of Justice.

Ministry of Justice/National Offender Management Service (2011). *Statistics on race and the criminal justice system 2010*. London, Ministry of Justice.

Mirza, H. S. (2006). Transcendence over diversity: black women in the academy. *Policy Futures in Education* 4(2): 101–133.

Modood, T. (1994). Political blackness and British Asians. *Sociology* 28(4): 859–876.

Moore, M. (2008). In France, prisons filled with Muslims. *Washington Post*, 29 April.

Mowatt, R. (2009). Notes from a leisure son: expanding an understanding of whiteness in leisure. *Journal of Leisure Research* 41(4): 511–528.

Mowatt, R., French, B. and Malebranche, D. (2013). Black/female/body hypervisibility and invisibility. *Journal of Leisure Research* 45(5): 644–660.

Mulkay, M. (1988). *On humour: its nature and place in modern society*. Cambridge, Polity Press.

Muller, F., Van Zoonen, L. and De Roode, L. (2007). Accidental racists: experiences and contradictions of racism in local Amsterdam soccer fan culture. *Soccer and Society* 8(2/3): 336–350.

Nadkarni, R. (2015). Why Missouri's football team joined a protest against school administration. *Sports Illustrated*, 9 November.

Nakamura, L. (2002). *Cybertypes: race, ethnicity, and identity on the internet*. London, Routledge.

National Centre for Social Research (2013). *30 years of British social attitudes self-reported racial prejudice data*. London, National Centre for Social Research.

Norman, L. (2010). Feeling second best. *Sociology of Sport* 27: 89–104.

Norman, L., North, J. K. H., Flintoff, A. and Rankin, A. J. (2014). *Sporting experiences and coaching aspirations among Black and Minority Ethnic (BME) groups*. Leeds, Sports Coach UK.

Norman, M. (2015). Sport in the underlife of a total institution: social control and resistance in Canadian prisons. *International Review for the Sociology of Sport* 52(5): 598–614.

Nwoye, I. C. (2014). Cycling on the sidewalk: the new stop-and-frisk? *Village Voice*, 30 October.

ONS (Office for National Statistics) (2011). Ethnicity and national identity in England and Wales: 2011. Retrieved 10 October 2017, from https://www.ons.gov.uk/peoplepopula tionandcommunity/culturalidentity/ethnicity/articles/ethnicityandnationalidentityinengla ndandwales/2012-12-11#key-points

Omi, M. and H. Winant (2002). Racial formation. *In: Race critical theories*, eds P. Essed and D. T. Goldberg. Oxford, Blackwell.

Ospina, S. and E. Foldy (2009). A critical review of race and ethnicity in the leadership litera-ture: surfacing context, power and the collective dimensions of leadership. *The Leadership Quarterly* 20: 876–896.

Ostrower, C. (2015). Humour as defense mechanism. *Interpretation: A Journal of Bible and Theology* 69(2): 183–195.

Ouseley, H. (1990). Resisting institutional change. *In: Race and local politics*, eds W. Ball and J. Solomos. London, Macmillan.

Parker, A., Meek, R. and Lewis, G. (2014). Sport in a youth prison: male young offenders' experiences of a sporting intervention. *Journal of Youth Studies* 17(3): 381–396.

Parker, L., Deyhle, D. and Villenas, S., eds (1999). *Race is … race isn't: critical race theory and qualitative studies in education*. Boulder CO, Westview Press.

Perakyla, A. (2005). Analyzing talk and text. *In: The Sage handbook of qualitative research*, eds N. Denzin and Y. Lincoln. London, Sage.

Phillip, S. (2000). Race and the pursuit of happiness. *Journal of Leisure Research* 32(1): 121–1224.

Phillips, C. (2012). *The multicultural prison: ethnicity, masculinity, and social relations among prisoners*. Oxford, Oxford University Press.

Phillips, C. and C. Webster, eds (2014). *New directions in race, ethnicity and crime*. London, Routledge.

Picca, L. H. and J. R. Feagin (2007). *Two-faced racism: whites in the backstage and frontstage*. New York and London, Routledge.

Pickering, M. (2008). *Blackface minstrelsy in Britain*. Aldershot, Ashgate.

Pierce, C. (1970). *Offensive mechanisms: the Black seventies*. Boston, Porter Sargent: 265–282.

Pierce, C., Carew, J., Pierce-Gonzalez, D. and Willis, D. (1978*). An experiment in racism: television and education*. Beverley Hills, Sage.

Poulton, E. and O. Durell (2014). Uses and meanings of 'Yid' in English football fandom: a case study of Tottenham Hotspur Football Club. *International Review for the Sociology of Sport* 16: 1–20.

Press Association (2015). African team MTN-Qhubeka complains of racism on tour of Austria. *Guardian*, 9 July.

Press Association (2017). Heather Rabbatts to stand down as a nonexecutive director of the FA. *Guardian*, 14 June.

Proxmire, D. (2008). Coaching diversity: the Rooney rule, its application and ideas for expansion. American Consitution Society for Law and Policy: 1–9. www.acslaw.org/ files/Proxmire%201ssue%20Brief.pdf

Puwar, N. (2004). *Race, gender and bodies out of place*. Oxford, Berg.

Quinton, P. (2015). Race, disproportionality and officer decision-making. *In: Stop and search: the anatomy of a police power*, eds R. Delsol and M. Shiner. Basingstoke, Palgrave Macmillan: 57–78.

Ratna, A. (2007). British Asian females' racialised and gendered experiences of identity and women's football. Ph.D. thesis, Chelsea School, University of Brighton.

Ratna, A. (2014). 'Who are ya?' The national identities and belongings of British Asian football fans. *Patterns of Prejudice* 48(3): 286–308.

Razack, S. (1999). *Looking white people in the eye: gender, race and culture in courtrooms and classrooms.* Toronto, University of Toronto Press.

Regan, M. and J. Feagin (2017). College sport leadership: systemic racial employment barriers. *In: Sport and discrimination*, eds D. Kilvington and J. Price. London, Routledge.

Reid, I. (2015). Just a wind-up? Ethnicity, religion and prejudice in Scottish football-related comedy. *International Review for the Sociology of Sport* 50(2): 227–245.

Ricciardelli, R. (2015). Establishing and asserting masculinity in Canadian penitentiaries. *Journal of Gender Studies* 24(2): 170–191.

Richardson, J. (2006). *Analysing newspapers: an approach from critical discourse analysis.* Basingstoke, Palgrave Macmillan.

Richmond, L. and C. Johnson (2009). 'It's a race war': race and leisure experiences in California State Prison. *Journal of Leisure Research* 41(4): 565–580.

Roberts, L. (2013). Becoming a black researcher: reflections on racialised identity and knowledge production. *International Review of Qualitative Inquiry* 6(3): 337–359.

Roberts, N. S. (2009). Crossing the color line with a different perspective on Whiteness and (anti)racism: a response to Mary McDonald. *Journal of Leisure Research* 41(4): 495–509.

Robidoux, M. (2004). Narratives of race relations in Southern Alberta: an examination of conflicting sporting practices. *Sociology of Sport* 21: 287–301.

Robidoux, M. (2012). *Stickhandling through the margins: First Nations hockey in Canada.* Toronto, University of Toronto Press.

Roithmayr, D. (2014). *Reproducing racism: how everyday choices lock in white advantage.* New York, New York University Press.

Rojek, C. (2005). *Leisure theory: principles and practice.* Basingstoke, Palgrave Macmillan.

Rollock, N. (2013). A political investment: revisiting race and racism in the research process. *Discourse: Studies in the Cultural Politics of Education* 34(4): 492–509.

Rollock, N. and D. Gillborn (2011). Critical race theory (CRT). BERA Online Resource. British Educational Resource Association. https://www.besa.org.uk/

Sabo, D. (2001). Doing time, doing masculinity. *In: Prison masculinities*, eds D. Sabo, T. Kupers and W. London. Philadelphia, Temple University Press.

Sabo, D., Kupers, T. and London, W. (2001). *Prison masculinities.* Philadelphia, Temple University Press.

Sakala, L. (2014). Breaking down mass incarceration in the 2010 Census: state-by-state incarceration rates by race/ethnicity. Retrieved 3 December 2014, from https://www.prisonpolicy.org/reports/rates.html

Salter, P. and G. Adams (2013). Toward a critical race psychology. *Social and Personality Psychology Compass* 7(11): 781–793.

Sanchez-Hucles, J. and D. Davis (2010). Women and women of color in leadership: complexity, identity, and intersectionality. *American Psychologist* 65(3): 171–181.

Satzewich, V. (2000). Whiteness limited: racialization and the social construction of 'peripheral Europeans'. *Social History* 66(33): 271–290.

Schuloff, A. (2015). More than Native American narratives: temporal shifting and authentic identities. *Narrative Inquiry* 25(1): 166–183.

Scraton, S. (2001). Reconceptualising 'race' gender and sport: the contribution of black feminism. *In: 'Race' sport and British society*, eds B. Carrington and I. McDonald. London, Routledge.

Seaton, M. (2009). Why is cycling such a white sport? *Guardian*, 10 August.

Service, M. N. O. M. (2011). *Physical education (PE) for prisoners.* London, Ministry of Justice.

Shaw, S. (2006). Scratching the back of 'Mr X': analyzing gendered social processes in sport organizations. *Journal of Sport Management* 20: 510–534.

Shenglan, C. and B. Kleiner (2003). Housing discrimination based on race. *Equal Opportunities International* 22(3): 16–48.

Sheriff, L. (2011). Steve Williams racism: Tiger Woods' former caddie apologises for 'racist' comment. *Huffington Post*, 5 November.

Sherwood, H. (2013a). Israel president demands crackdown on racism in football. *Guardian*, 29 January.

Sherwood, H. (2013b). Israelis shocked by racist football chants bringing shame to a once proud team. *Guardian*, 9 February.

Shipman, T. and S. Griffiths (2016). A young black man is more likely to be in prison than at a top university. *Sunday Times*, 31 January.

Shuford, J. (2001). Four Du Boisian contributions to critical race theory. *Transactions of the Charles S. Peirce Society* 37(3): 301–337.

Silver, D. (2000). Margins in the wires: looking for race, gender, and sexuality in the Blacksburg electronic village. In: *Race in cyberspace*, eds B. Kolko, L. Nakamura and G. Rodman. London, Routledge.

Smith, E. and A. Hattery (2011). Race relations theories: implications for sport management. *Journal of Sport Management* 25: 107–117.

Snyder, E. (1991). Sociology of sport and humour. *International Review for the Sociology of Sport* 26(2): 119–131.

Solorzano, D. (2013). *Critical race theory part I.* California, Saint Mary's College.

Solorzano, D., Miguel, C. and Yosso, T. (2000). Critical race theory, racial microaggressions, and campus racial climate: the experiences of African American college students. *Journal of Negro Education* 69(1/2): 60–73.

Sporting Equals (2016). *Who's on board in sport?* Birmingham, Sporting Equals.

Spracklen, K., Hylton, K. and Long, J. (2006). Managing and monitoring equality and diversity in UK sport: an evaluation of the Sporting Equals Racial Equality Standard and its impact on organisational change. *Journal of Sport and Social Issues* 30(3): 289–305.

Spracklen, K., Long, J. and Hylton, K. (2014). Leisure opportunities and new migrant communities: challenging the contribution of sport. *Leisure Studies* 40(11): 1779–1797.

Staff, J. (2016). This one stat reveals the sharing economy's racism problem. *Time*, 14 December.

Stark, T. (2015). Understanding the selection bias: social network processes and the effect of prejudice on the avoidance of outgroup friends. *Social Psychology Quarterly* 78(2): 127–150.

Starn, O. (2011). *The passion of Tiger Woods.* Durham NC, Duke University Press.

Steinbach, R., Green, J., Datta, J. and Edwards, P. (2011). Cycling and the city: a case study of how gendered, ethnic and class identities can shape healthy transport choices. *Social Science and Medicine* 72: 1123–1130.

Sue, D. (2003). *Overcoming our racism: the journey to liberation.* San Francisco, Jossey-Bass.

Sue, D. (2010a). An introduction. In: *Microaggressions, marginality, and oppression*, eds D. Sue. New Jersey, Wiley.

Sue, D. (2010b). *Microaggressions in everyday life: race, gender and sexual orientation.* New Jersey, Wiley.

Sue, D., Bucceri, J., Lin, A., Nadal, K. and Torino, G. (2007). Racial microaggressions and the Asian American experience. *Cultural Diversity and Ethnic Minority Psychology* 13(1): 72–81.

Sue, D., Capodilipo, C., Torino, G., Bucceri, J., Holder, A., Nadal, K. and Esquilin, M. (2007). Racial microaggressions in everyday life: implications for clinical practice. *American Psychologist* 62(4): 271–286.

Sullivan, P. (2013). Humor styles as a predictor of satisfaction within sport teams. *Humor* 26(2): 343–349.

Sullivan, S. and N. Tuana, eds (2007). *Race and epistemologies of ignorance*. Albany, State University of New York Press.

Tate, S. (2016). 'I can't quite put my finger on it': racism's touch. *Ethnicities* 16(1): 68–85.

Testa, A. and M. Amara, eds (2016). *Sport in Islam and in Muslim communities*. London, Routledge.

Tranby, E. and D. Hartmann (2008). Critical whiteness theories and the evangelical 'race problem': extending Emerson and Smith's 'Divided by Faith'. *Journal for the Scientific Study of Religion* 47(3): 341–359.

Trepagnier, B. (2010). *Silent racism: how well-meaning white people perpetuate the racial divide*. Boulder CO and London, Paradigm Publishers.

Tuhiwai Smith, L. (2012). *Decolonizing methodologies: research and indigenous peoples*. London and New York, University of Otago Press.

UN (2005). *Dimensions of racism*. New York and Geneva, United Nations: 199.

UN (2013). The UN and antiracism in sport. Retrieved 14 September 2014, from www.ohchr.org/EN/NewsEvents/IDERD/Pages/EliminationRacialDiscrimination.aspx

UNESCO (1978). Declaration on race and racial prejudice. Paris, UNESCO.

United Nations (1955). Standard minimum rules for the treatment of prisoners. Retrieved 29 December 2016, from www.ohchr.org/Documents/ProfessionalInterest/treatmentprisoners.pdf

van Sterkenburg, J., Knoppers, A. and Leeuw, S. (2010). Race, ethnicity, and content analysis of the sports media: a critical reflection. *Media, Culture and Society* 32(4): 819–839.

Vizenor, G. (1994). Trickster discourse: comic and tragic themes in Native American literature. *In: Buried roots and indestructible seeds: the survival of American Indian life in story, history, and spirit*, eds M. Lindquist and M. Zanger. Wisconsin, University of Wisconsin Press.

Walmsley, R. (2016). *World prison population list* (11th edn). London, Institute for Criminal Policy Research: 1–15.

Walseth, K. (2016). Sport and integration discourse in Norway: how do policy makers perceive and respond to the sporting needs of Muslim communities? *In: Sport in Islam and in Muslim Communities*, eds A. Testa and M. Amara. London, Routledge.

Warde, B. (2012). Black male disproportionality in the criminal justice systems of the USA, Canada, and England: a comparative analysis of incarceration. *Journal of African American Studies* 17: 461–479.

Watson, C. (2015). A sociologist walks into a bar (and other academic challenges): towards a methodology of humour. *Sociology* 49(3): 407–421.

Weaver, S. (2010a). Developing a rhetorical analysis of racist humour: examining anti-black jokes on the internet. *Social Semiotics* 20(5): 535–555.

Weaver, S. (2010b). The 'other' laughs back: humour and resistance in anti-racist comedy. *Sociology* 44(1): 31–48.

Weaver, S. (2011a). Jokes, rhetoric and embodied racism: a rhetorical discourse analysis of the logics of racist jokes on the internet. *Ethnicities* 11(4): 413–435.

Weaver, S. (2011b). *The rhetoric of racist humour*. Farnham, Ashgate.

Weise, E. (2016). Airbnb taps Holder to take on discrimination. *USA Today*, 21 July.

Werbner, P. and T. Modood (1997). *Debating cultural hybridity: multi-cultural identities and the politics of anti-racism*. London and Atlantic Highlands NJ, Zed Books.

West, C. (2001). *Race matters*. Boston, Beacon Press.

Western, S. (2013). *Leadership: a critical text*. London, Sage.

Westwood, S. (1990). Racism, black masculinity and space. *In: Men, masculinities and social theory*, eds J. Hearn and D. Morgan. London, Unwin Hyman.

Whine, M. (1997). The far right on the internet. *In: The governance of cyberspace*, ed. B. Loader. London, Routledge: 209–227.

White, N. (2010). Indigenous Australian women's leadership: stayin' strong against the post-colonial tide. *International Journal of Leadership in Education: Theory and Practice* 13(1): 7–25.

Whitson, D. (1990). Sport in the social construction of masculinity. *Sport, men and the gender order: critical feminist perspectives*. M. Messner and D. Sabo. Champaign IL, Human Kinetics.

Wilkins, J. and A. Eisenbraun (2009). Humor theories and the physiological benefits of laughter. *Holistic Nursing Practice* (November/December): 349–354.

Williams, P. J. (1997). *Seeing a colour-blind future: the paradox of race*. London, Virago Press.

Williams, S. (2009). *My life: queen of the court*. London, Pocket Book.

Winant, H. (2001). *The world is a ghetto: race and democracy since world war II*. New York, Basic Books.

Winant, H. (2004). *The new politics of race: globalism, difference, justice*. Minneapolis and London, University of Minnesota Press.

Wing, A. K. (2003). *Critical race feminism: a reader*. New York and London, New York University Press.

Winograd, K. (2011). Sports biographies of African American football players: the racism of colorblindness in children's literature. *Race, Ethnicity and Education* 14(3): 331–349.

Wisniewski, M. (2017). Biking while black. *Chicago Tribune*, 17 March.

Yosso, T. (2005). Whose culture has capital? A critical race theory discussion of community cultural wealth. *Race, Ethnicity and Education* 8(1): 69–91.

Young, J. (2001). Scholars question the image of the internet as a race-free utopia. *Chronicle of Higher Education* 48(5): 2–3.

Zamudio, M. M., Russell, C., Rios, F. A. and Bridgeman, J. L. (2011). *Critical race theory matters: education and ideology*. London, Routledge.

Zirin, D. (2007). *Welcome to the terrordome: the pain, politics, and promise of sports*. Illinois, Haymarket Books.

INDEX

Note: bold indicates tables; 'n' indicates chapter notes.